SOCIAL WORK AND CRIMINAL JUSTICE:

VOLUME 7

THE PROCESS AND OUTCOMES OF COMMUNITY BASED THROUGHCARE

Gill McIvor

Monica Barry

Social Work Research Centre
Department of Applied Social Science
University of Stirling

THE SCOTTISH OFFICE CENTRAL RESEARCH UNIT
1998

ACKNOWLEDGEMENTS

Since its inception in the Spring of 1994, this research project has received a great deal of the time, energy, cooperation and enthusiasm of many clients, social workers and managers in the areas which participated in the study.

We would like to acknowledge their support and that received from the Scottish Office Home Department, in particular from Dr Fiona Paterson, Principal Research Officer in the Central Research Unit. We are also grateful for the assistance of the Scottish Criminal Record Office in providing access to data required.

Special thanks are due to Vivien Campbell, freelance researcher, for assisting in the data collection and, in particular, for her perseverance in tracking down respondents in one of the study areas. Thanks also to Pam Lavery and Trish Hughes for their patience in deciphering the endless transcripts, and their tolerance in ignoring some of the more colourful language used - especially by the clients!

Gill McIvor
Monica Barry
1998

SOCIAL WORK AND CRIMINAL JUSTICE
RESEARCH PROGRAMME REPORTS

Paterson, F. and Tombs, J. (1998)

Social Work and Criminal Justice: Volume 1 - *The Impact of Policy.* The Stationery Office.

Phase One:

McAra, L. (1998)

Social Work and Criminal Justice: Volume 2 - *Early Arrangements.* The Stationery Office.

Phase Two:

Brown, L., Levy, L. and McIvor, G. (1998)

Social Work and Criminal Justice: Volume 3 - *The National and Local Context.* The Stationery Office.

Brown, L., Levy, L. (1998)

Social Work and Criminal Justice: Volume 4 - *Sentencer Decision Making.* The Stationery Office.

McAra, L. (1998a)

Social Work and Criminal Justice: Volume 5 - *Parole Board Decision Making.* The Stationery Office.

McIvor, G. and Barry, M. (1998)

Social Work and Criminal Justice: Volume 6 - *Probation.* The Stationery Office.

McIvor, G. and Barry, M. (1998a)

Social Work and Criminal Justice: Volume 7 - *Community Based Throughcare.* The Stationery Office.

THE SCOTTISH OFFICE CENTRAL RESEARCH UNIT

Social Work
Research Findings No. 19

Social Work and Criminal Justice: Community-Based Throughcare

Gill McIvor and Monica Barry

National Objectives and Standards for Social Work Services in the Criminal Justice System and the 100% funding initiative ('the policy') were introduced in 1991 in order to secure the provision of services which have the confidence of both criminal justice decision-makers and the wider public. This study is part of the social research programme designed to evaluate policy implementation. The aim of this study is to examine the process and outcomes of community-based throughcare.

Main findings

■ Whilst offending behaviour was the issue most often identified as being significant by social workers, ex-prisoners were thought most likely to attach importance to accommodation and employment.

■ Social workers believed that they had made greatest progress in relation to addressing alcohol use, the provision of general practical support and helping ex-prisoners to resettle in the community.

■ Social workers believed that two-thirds of ex-prisoners in the study sample were unlikely to reoffend, a quarter were thought fairly likely to reoffend and in one in nine cases, further offending was considered very likely.

■ Community-based throughcare was viewed as less helpful than it might be by released prisoners and was acknowledged by social work managers to be the least well developed of the 100 per cent funded services.

---

1 National Standards for Community Service had been introduced in 1989.

1998

Introduction

The National Objectives and Standards (the Standards, 1991) set out in a framework within which social work are required to provide services where costs are met by the 100 per cent funding initiative (initially, social enquiry reports and associated court services, community service, probation, parole and other aspects of throughcare).

Prior to the development of the Standards, local authorities had to fund most social work services out of their general income. Criminal justice services were, therefore, in competition for resources with other local authority services and as a result were not always of sufficient quantity and quality to meet the requirements of the courts.

The main aims of the policy are:

- to reduce the use of custody by increasing the availability, improving the quality and targeting the use of community-based court disposals on those most at risk of custody, especially young offenders;

- to enable offenders to address their offending behaviour and make a successful adjustment to law-abiding life.

The purpose of this study was to examine the process and outcomes of community-based throughcare. Four social work authorities were selected for study, to reflect areas with urban centres, those which were predominantly rural and to represent both specialist and more generic forms of organising social work criminal justice services.

The research focused upon all throughcare cases from these authorities which closed between 1 July 1994 and 30 April 1995. Also included were life licencees who, though still subject to statutory supervision, had been released from custody since April 1992. Information was obtained from 60 social work files from 48 questionnaires completed by social workers and from interviews with 31 ex-prisoners.

Community-based throughcare

Most ex-prisoners on statutory supervision were seen by their supervising social worker within 24 hours of their release and ex-prisoners who received voluntary assistance made contact, on average, six weeks after being released from custody. However, Standards for contact beyond the initial meeting were not always met for ex-prisoners on statutory supervision.

The majority of services provided both at the pre-release stage and following release focused upon practical issues such as accommodation, financial matters and employment. The majority of work was undertaken on an individual basis and, with the exception of employment services and services for offenders with alcohol or drugs problems, most work was undertaken by the supervising social worker.

Social workers' views

Whilst offending behaviour was the issue most often identified as being significant by social workers, ex-prisoners were thought most likely to attach importance to accommodation and employment. Objectives which were related to helping ex-prisoners resettle in the community, offending behaviour and addressing alcohol abuse were most often achieved. Social workers had least success in dealing with problematic drug use, helping prisoners to obtain accommodation and providing them with emotional support.

Two-thirds of ex-prisoners in the sample were believed unlikely to reoffend, a quarter were thought fairly likely to reoffend and in one in nine cases, further offending was considered very unlikely. Younger offenders and offenders subject to voluntary supervision were thought more often to present a risk of continued offending. Risk of reoffending was indicated by: continued offending during the period on throughcare; the existence of problematic alcohol or drug use or other factors associated with offending; or by general instability in ex-prisoners' lives.

Forty-four per cent of the sample were considered by their social workers to be less at risk of reoffending on termination of supervision compared with when they were released from custody. In two-thirds of these cases, it was suggested that ex-prisoners had gained further insight into their offending behaviour and its consequences since being released from prison.

Ex-prisoners' views

Just over two-thirds of ex-prisoners had received one or more visits from their community-based social worker in prison; and just over a third recalled having had a three-way meeting with the prison-based and community-based social workers.

Nine prisoners interviewed believed that their situation had improved as a direct result of social work advice or intervention but the remaining interviewees thought that their circumstances had not improved or, if they had, that they themselves had achieved the change on their own.

The majority of ex-prisoners in the sample thought it unlikely that they would reoffend and only six believed that reoffending was likely. Throughcare was perceived to have had some impact on the likelihood of reoffending by 42 per cent of the sample.

Conclusion

Community-based throughcare was viewed as less helpful than it might be by released prisoners and was acknowledged by social work managers to be the least well developed of the 100 per cent funded services.

What appears to be required to improve the quality and effectiveness of throughcare is:

- greater clarity about the objectives of throughcare practice;

- an adequate level of resourcing;

- a clearer distinction between the role of prison-based and community-based social work staff in the period prior to release;

- improved communication and co-ordination between prison-based and community-based social workers;

- a longer time lapse between prisoners' notification of parole being granted and their release date;

- a more consistent emphasis upon the practical needs of prisoners on release.

The study was carried out by the Social Work Research Centre at Stirling University as part of the programme of research to evaluate social work criminal justice policy. The research programme was conducted by The Scottish Office Central Research Unit in collaboration with the Social Work Research Centre at Stirling University and with Edinburgh University. It was funded by the Home Department of The Scottish Office.

Social Work and Criminal Justice Volume 7: 'Community-Based Throughcare'; the report of the research programme summarised in this Research Findings is published by The Stationery Office. It may be purchased from The Stationery Office, price £14 per copy.

Reports of Individual Studies on this programme are also available:

Social Work and Criminal Justice Volume 1: 'The Impact of Policy'.
Social Work and Criminal Justice Volume 2: 'Early Arrangements'.
Social Work and Criminal Justice Volume 3: 'The National and Local Context'.
Social Work and Criminal Justice Volume 4: 'Sentencer Decision-Making'.
Social Work and Criminal Justice Volume 5: 'Parole Board Decision-Making'.
Social Work and Criminal Justice Volume 6: 'Probation'.

Cheques should be made payable to The Stationery Office and addressed to:

The Stationery Office Ltd, Mail Order Department, 21 South Gyle Crescent, Edinburgh, EH12 9EB. Telephone: 0131-479-3141 or Fax 0131-479-3142.

The following Research Findings for other studies on this programme are also available:

Findings 13: 'The Impact of Policy'
Findings 14: 'Early Arrangements'.
Findings 15: 'The National and Local Context'.
Findings 16: 'Sentencer Decision-Making'.
Findings 17: 'Parole Board Decision-Making'.
Findings 18: 'Probation'.

Research Findings may be photocopied, or further copies may be obtained from:

The Scottish Office Central Research Unit

Room 53

James Craig Walk

Edinburgh EH1 3BA

or

Telephone: 0131-244-5397

Fax: 0131-244-5393

ISBN 0-7480-6665-9

THE SCOTTISH OFFICE

Designed and produced on behalf of The Scottish Office by The Stationery Office J16005 1/98

9 780748 066650

CONTENTS

SUMMARY

INTRODUCTION

The Policy

In Scotland, statutory social work services to offenders and their families are provided by the local authority social work departments. Since April 1991, the Scottish Office has reimbursed to social work departments the full costs of providing a range of statutory social work services in the criminal justice system. National Objectives and Standards (the National Standards) were introduced by the Social Work Services Group of the Scottish Office to coincide with the introduction of the funding initiative.

The National Standards and the funding initiative cover: social enquiry reports; court social work services; probation; community service; and throughcare (social work in prisons is funded by the Scottish Prison Service). Since 1991, the initiative has been extended to supervised release orders, bail information and accommodation schemes, and supervised attendance order schemes (the latter two schemes are not yet available on a national basis).

The main aims of the Government's policy are:

- to reduce the use of custody by increasing the availability, improving the quality and targeting the use of community based court disposals and throughcare services on those most at risk of custody, especially young adult repeat offenders;

- to enable offenders to address their offending behaviour and make a successful adjustment to law abiding life.

Background to the Research

Central Government's review and evaluation of implementation of the funding initiative and the National Standards involves a programme of inspection by Social Work Services Inspectorate (SWSI), interpretation of statistics and a programme of research.

The research programme examines progress towards policy objectives. Four sheriff court areas, each in separate social work authorities, were selected as study sites for Phase Two of the research programme to reflect areas of both high and low population density and to represent both specialist and more generic forms of organising social work criminal justice services. The names of the four areas have been anonymised in reports and are referred to as Scott, Wallace, Burns and Bruce.

The present study examines the process and outcomes of community based throughcare services following the introduction of 100 per cent funding and National Standards. It seeks to describe the characteristics of ex-prisoners subject to different throughcare arrangements; to document the services offered by community based social workers and the framework within which they are provided; and to examine the effectiveness of community based throughcare in addressing ex-prisoners' needs and assisting in their resettlement in the community.

In three of the four study authorities throughcare cases for inclusion in the sample were drawn from across the region as a whole. This step was taken to maximise the number of cases which could be identified within a given period of time. In the fourth area the focus was upon throughcare cases dealt with by two area teams in the district, including those held by a dedicated throughcare project (funded by the Urban Renewal Unit) which offered a service to offenders from areas of priority treatment (APTs) across the district.

The total possible sample consisted of all throughcare cases (parole, statutory aftercare and voluntary aftercare) which closed between 1 July 1994 and 30 April 1995 and which related to prisoners who had been released from custody since April 1992 (when the National Standards for throughcare came into effect). Also included were life licencees who, though still subject to statutory supervision, had been released from custody since April 1992. Information was obtained in the main from social work files, from questionnaires completed by social workers in individual cases and from interviews with ex-prisoners.

CHARACTERISTICS OF THE SAMPLE

More than two-thirds of the sample of 60 ex-prisoners were subject to parole and just over half of this group had additional requirements attached to their licences by the Parole Board. Additional requirements most frequently related to drug or alcohol counselling, residence and treatment for sexual offending. Most of the additional requirements in respect of drug counselling pertained to offenders who had been sentenced for offences involving drugs. Parolees in Bruce were most likely to have additional requirements attached to their licences. Most parole licences were for durations of up to 12 months. The average period on licence was highest in Scott and lowest in Bruce.

The average length of determinate sentence imposed was 40 months. Ex-prisoners in receipt of voluntary assistance on release had served, on average, shorter sentences than those subject to statutory supervision. The majority of the sample were males over 20 years of age. Life licencees were older, on average, than other groups of former prisoners.

The majority of ex-prisoners had one or more previous convictions and just over half had previously served a custodial sentence. Just under a third of prisoners in receipt of community based throughcare had been subject to supervision through the children's hearing system and more than a third had previous experience of community based social work disposals. Ex-prisoners in receipt of voluntary assistance had more extensive criminal histories, on average, than did those who were subject to statutory supervision on release.

THE THROUGHCARE PROCESS

Contacts with Social Workers

Twenty-nine ex-prisoners had received a visit from their community based social worker while in custody and in 31 cases supervising social workers had established contact with prisoners' families, usually in connection with the preparation of a home circumstances report for the Parole Board. Most ex-prisoners on statutory supervision were seen by their supervising social worker within 24 hours of their release. Ex-prisoners who received voluntary assistance made contact, on average, six weeks after being released from custody.

Prisoners subject to statutory supervision had more contacts with their social workers than did those in receipt of voluntary assistance. Ex-prisoners in Scott had more office contacts with their social workers in the first three months of supervision and had slightly more contacts overall during this period than did those in the other areas. National Standards with respect to the frequency of contact in the first three months and the date of initial contact with statutory throughcare cases were more often met in Scott than in the other study areas.

Reviews

Formal reviews were held in 29 cases with just over half of these former prisoners having a single review. Initial reviews were conducted, on average, 17 weeks after the prisoner's release. Few reviews resulted in amendments to the objectives of supervision. Reviews in Scott were most likely to be attended by the social worker's first line manager and this was least likely to occur in Wallace.

Objectives and Services Provided

The majority of services provided both at the pre-release stage and following release focused upon practical issues such as accommodation, financial matters and employment. The majority of work was undertaken on a one-to-one basis and, with the exception of employment services and services for offenders with problems related to the use of alcohol or drugs, most work was undertaken by the supervising social workers themselves.

There were some variations in the services provided and objectives pursued across the study areas. Work in Scott, for example, more often focused on employment and accommodation, while the broader aim of re-settling the offender in the community was most prevalent in Bruce, and social workers in Wallace were most likely to focus upon offending behaviour.

Accommodation featured most often as an objective with voluntary cases. Work with life licencees was most clearly focused upon practical issues associated with the re-integration of the ex-prisoner in the community, while objectives pursued and services provided in respect of parolees with additional requirements most often focused upon offending behaviour, alcohol and drug abuse, suggesting that this category of ex-prisoner was perceived as presenting the greatest risk of further offending on release.

THE OUTCOMES OF THROUGHCARE

Few ex-prisoners received formal warnings while subject to supervision and only two were recalled to prison as a consequence of further offending: both, significantly in view of the previous argument, were parolees with additional requirements attached to their licences. Eight individuals were reconvicted of offences committed while in receipt of community based throughcare and one had been charged with an offence allegedly committed during this period. Young offenders were more likely than adults to have been reconvicted and those who were reconvicted had more serious offending histories as evidenced by the number of previous convictions and previous custodial sentences. Voluntary assistance was terminated in most instances because outstanding issues had been addressed or because the ex-prisoner ceased to maintain contact with the social work department.

There was some evidence of an improvement in ex-prisoners' social circumstances - as indicated by changes in living arrangements and employment status - following the period of community based throughcare.

SOCIAL WORKERS' VIEWS OF THE EFFECTIVENESS OF THROUGHCARE

Objectives

Avoiding or addressing offending featured as an objective in just over three-fifths of the 48 cases in which social workers completed questionnaires. This was followed by employment/education, accommodation, helping the offender to resettle in the community, alcohol and family relationships. Social workers appeared to make greatest progress in relation to alcohol use, the provision of general practical support and helping ex-prisoners to resettle in the community. They had least success in dealing with problematic drug use, helping ex-prisoners to obtain accommodation and providing them with emotional support.

Responses to Throughcare

The majority of ex-prisoners were said by social workers to have been motivated to address their offending and other problems and three-quarters of the sample were believed to have responded positively to throughcare. Factors which were believed by social workers to have adversely affected ex-prisoners' responses to throughcare included the existence of social or personal problems which detracted from the ex-prisoner's ability or willingness to comply; reluctance on the part of the offender to engage with the social worker; the personal characteristics of the offender; and the influence of offending peers. Ex-prisoners' responses to throughcare were believed by their social workers to have been influenced positively by their motivation to avoid further offending and its consequences; by stability in their lives; and by features of the throughcare contact itself - the help received, the relationship established with the social worker or the clear framework provided by a statutory licence.

Likelihood of Re-offending

Two thirds of ex-prisoners were believed unlikely to re-offend, a quarter were thought fairly likely to re-offend and in one in nine cases further offending was considered very likely. Offenders who were described as highly motivated to address their offending and other problems were least likely to be considered at some risk of committing offences in future. Risk of continued offending was indicated by continued offending during the period on throughcare, by the existence of problematic alcohol or drug use or other factors associated with offending or by general instability in the ex-prisoners' lives. By contrast, in providing reasons why ex-prisoners were unlikely to re-offend social workers made reference to the isolated nature of the original offence or the time that had elapsed since its commission; offenders' motivation to avoid offending and its consequences; the stability of the ex-prisoner's circumstances; and improvements in the offender's circumstances since the commission of the original offence.

Forty-four per cent of the sample were considered by their social workers to be less at risk of re-offending compared with when they were released from custody, while in 48 per cent of cases the risk of recidivism was thought not to have changed.

Most offenders whose risk of recidivism was thought not to have changed were not considered to be at risk of further offending. Increased self-awareness appeared to be the key factor which distinguished those whose risk of re-offending remained low throughout and those whose risk had decreased since returning to the community. Overall, throughcare was thought to have contributed to a reduced risk of re-offending in approximately 40 per cent of cases in the sample.

EX-PRISONERS' EXPERIENCES AND VIEWS OF THROUGHCARE

Effectiveness of Throughcare

Most of those subject to release on licence had high expectations of the social work support they might receive though seven saw parole as merely a monitoring or surveillance exercise.

Although some of the 31 respondents were able to cite examples of constructive help they had received from prison based social workers, most viewed prison social work input as unhelpful, either because social workers were seen as untrustworthy or uninterested or because the insular or detached nature of prison life made prison social workers less effective in liaising with the outside world.

Views were mixed as to the helpfulness of visits in prison from their community based social worker, with some indicating that they would have welcomed more assistance in relation to housing on release. Most ex-prisoners who had had no contact with their community based social worker prior to release would have valued such contact.

Respondents were generally of the view that there was agreement between themselves and their social workers as to what constituted the most pressing issues to address following release. The areas in which the greatest divergence of views was thought to exist were accommodation and offending behaviour: social workers, it was suggested, tended to underestimate the significance of the former and overplay the importance of the latter. Overall, nine ex-prisoners believed that their situation had improved as a direct result of social work advice or intervention but 22 thought that their circumstances had not improved or, if they had, that they themselves had achieved the change on their own.

Risk of Re-offending

Only seven offenders believed that offending might still be a problem which they wanted to address on release. Others felt that offending was an irrelevant issue frequently raised by the social worker, though nine ex-prisoners did not recall having discussed it at all. The majority of ex-prisoners thought it unlikely that they would re-offend and most believed that they were at less risk of re-offending compared with when they were first released from custody. Throughcare was believed to have had some impact on the likelihood of re-offending by 42 per cent of the sample. Other factors which had impacted positively upon the risk of recidivism included offenders' own motivation to avoid further offending and the significance of family and other personal relationships. More generally, ex-prisoners pointed to increased stability in their lives in areas such as employment or education, social contacts, increased maturity and control over former misuse of alcohol or drugs, issues which had similarly been stressed as significant by social workers.

Around two-thirds believed that their social worker had been helpful overall but just under a third felt that their involvement with social workers was too intrusive and time-consuming. Almost two-thirds of the sample felt they had gained nothing from the experience of throughcare. Just under half would have welcomed more proactive, practical support, particularly in relation to issues such as accommodation and employment.

CONCLUSION

It is concluded that effective pockets of throughcare practice do exist. However, community based throughcare was viewed as less helpful than it might be by released prisoners and was acknowledged by social work managers to be the least well developed of the 100 per cent funded services. What appears to be required to improve the quality and effectiveness of community based throughcare is:

* greater clarity regarding the objectives of throughcare practice (including the distinction between managing risk to the public and addressing offending behaviour);

* a level of resourcing which accurately reflects the requirements of an effective and comprehensive throughcare service;

* a clearer distinction between the role of prison based and community based social work staff in the period prior to release;

* improved communication and co-ordination between prison based and community based social workers;

* a longer time lapse between prisoners' notification of parole being granted and their release date;

* a more consistent emphasis upon the practical needs of prisoners on release.

CHAPTER ONE

INTRODUCTION AND METHODOLOGY

INTRODUCTION

In Scotland, statutory social work services to offenders and their families are provided by the local authority social work departments. Since April 1991, the Scottish Office has reimbursed to social work departments the full costs of providing a range of statutory social work services in the criminal justice system. National Objectives and Standards (the National Standards) were introduced by the Social Work Services Group of the Scottish Office to coincide with the introduction of the funding initiative. The aim of the National Standards is to promote the development of high quality management and practice, the most efficient and effective use of resources and to provide social work services to the criminal justice system which have the confidence of both the courts and the wider public.

The National Standards and the funding initiative cover: social enquiry reports; court social work services; probation; community service[1]; and throughcare (social work in prisons is funded by the Scottish Prison Service). Since 1991, the initiative has been extended to supervised release orders, bail information and accommodation schemes, and supervised attendance order schemes (the latter two schemes are not yet available on a national basis). It is intended to include diversion from prosecution in the 100 per cent funding arrangement, subject to the progress of pilot schemes established in 1996. At present, fine supervision, means enquiry reports and deferred sentence supervision are not included in the funding initiative.

Prior to the introduction of the 100 per cent funding initiative and the National Standards, local authorities had to fund the majority of social work services out of their general income. Criminal justice services were, therefore, in competition for resources with other local authority services and as a result were not always of sufficient quantity and quality to meet the requirements of the courts.

The main aims of the Government's policy are[2]:

- to reduce the use of custody by increasing the availability, improving the quality and targeting the use of community based court disposals and throughcare services on those most at risk of custody, especially young adult repeat offenders;

- to enable offenders to address their offending behaviour and make a successful adjustment to law abiding life.

BACKGROUND TO THE RESEARCH

Central Government's review and evaluation of implementation of the funding initiative and the National Standards involves a programme of inspection by Social Work Services Inspectorate (SWSI), interpretation of statistics and a programme of research.

The research programme is being conducted in three phases. The main purpose of Phase One, which was undertaken in 1992-1993, was to examine the responses of key criminal justice decision makers and Scottish Office officials to the principal objectives of the policy and the early arrangements for its implementation (McAra, 1998). Phase Two (of which this study is a part) consists of five inter-related studies, conducted in 1994-1995, which examine progress towards policy objectives: the national and local context of policy implementation (Brown, Levy and McIvor, 1998); sentencer decision making (Brown and Levy, 1998); Parole Board decision making (McAra, 1998a); the process and outcomes of probation (McIvor and Barry, 1998); and the process and outcomes of throughcare (McIvor and Barry, 1998a). Phase Three will look at the longer term impact of services for offenders.

Four sheriff court areas each in separate social work authorities were selected as study sites for the research programme to reflect areas of both high and low population density and to represent both specialist and more generic forms of organising social work criminal justice services. The names of the four areas have been anonymised in reports and are referred to as Scott, Wallace, Burns and Bruce.

---

[1] The 100% funding initiative and National Objectives and Standards were first applied to community service in 1989.
[2] Evaluation Strategy Working Group, September 1990. More recent statements (the 1996 White Paper on Crime and Punishment, paragraphs 9.1 and 10.3) are consistent with these aims.

The new arrangements were intended to promote and enhance the range and quality of community based social work disposals available to the courts and, in relation to throughcare, "to provide and facilitate services for prisoners, and their families, to help prepare them for release from custody and to help them resettle in the community on release within the law" (SWSG, 1991, para 12.6).

Prison based social work services are funded in full by the Scottish Prison Service (SPS). The joint SPS/SWSG document *Continuity through Co-operation* (1990) provides policy and practice guidance for the prison based contribution to the throughcare process and should, SWSG (1991) suggest, be read in conjunction with the National Standards for throughcare services.

The present study examines the process and outcomes of community based throughcare services following the introduction of 100 per cent funding and National Standards. It seeks to describe the characteristics of ex-prisoners subject to different throughcare arrangements; to document the services offered by community based social workers and the framework within which they are provided; and to examine the effectiveness of community based throughcare in addressing ex-prisoners' needs and assisting in their resettlement in the community.

More specifically, the study aims to:

- examine the services and resources provided by local authorities and the independent sector;

- examine the degree of cooperation between local authorities and independent sector service providers in the development and provision of services for individual offenders;

- consider the impact of strategic and organisational issues on the development and delivery of services to individual offenders;

- identify the relationship between release packages and the characteristics of individual offenders;

- examine how release packages and conditions inserted into parole and life licences are translated into practice and identify the frequency, location and type of contact with offenders and their families;

- examine the conclusions and recommendations of review reports to assess social worker and (where applicable) Parole Board views of progress;

- consider the impact of supervision on offenders' adherence to licence conditions and identify reasons for non-compliance and action taken, including (where applicable) decisions to recall the offender;

- examine the views of social workers, other service providers and offenders on their experience of throughcare services including the effectiveness of different forms of supervision in assisting the offender to re-integrate into the community, to tackle behaviour associated with offending and to address any problems the offender may have;

- examine the impact of throughcare on offenders' attitudes towards their offending behaviour and on their re-offending during the period of supervision.

The National Standards for throughcare services relate to two distinct groups of prisoners: those who are subject to statutory supervision on release from custody and those who request assistance from the social work department on a voluntary basis within 12 months of release. When the throughcare standards were introduced, social work departments were responsible for the supervision of parolees and of young offenders, aged between 16 and 20 years, who were subject to statutory aftercare following a period of detention in a young offenders institution. All young offenders sentenced to periods of detention of between six and 18 months were subject to a period of mandatory supervision for six months after their release while those detained for 18 months or more were, unless granted parole, on statutory aftercare licence for 12 months.

Any prisoner sentenced to a term of imprisonment or detention of 18 months or more could apply for parole after serving 12 months or one third of their sentence - whichever was the longer. Unless parole was granted, prisoners would normally be released after serving two-thirds of their sentence. Adults granted parole and released early would be subject to statutory supervision until the date on which they would have been released had parole not been granted by the Parole Board. Young offenders granted parole would be subject to supervision in the community for 12 months or until the expiry of sentence, whichever was the longer. In addition to general requirements to be of good behaviour, to keep in touch with the supervising officer and to inform the supervisor at once of any change of employment or address, additional requirements could be inserted into parole and statutory aftercare licences.

These provisions applied to prisoners serving determinate sentences. Prisoners who are serving indeterminate sentences - that is, who have been given life sentences or have been ordered to be detained during Her Majesty's pleasure - can only be released at the discretion of the Secretary of State following a recommendation for release by the Parole Board. These prisoners are subject to life licences, with the possibility of recall to prison for further offending, and are required to be supervised by the social work department for a minimum period of 10 years following their release.

Prison based and community based social workers have a key role in assisting the Parole Board's decision whether or not to grant early release on parole. Prison based social workers are required to provide a report for the parole dossier which assesses the risk of further offending on release, taking into account the prisoner's experience of imprisonment. Community based social workers are required to report on the likely level and nature of supervision and support which could be provided to the prisoner on release and to contribute to the assessment of risk of re-offending or social breakdown by the prisoner.

Ex-prisoners who were subject to parole or statutory licence aftercare could be recalled to prison if they were convicted of a further offence or if they otherwise failed to comply with the requirements of the licence. Young offenders subject to statutory aftercare could be recalled for a period of up to three months. Parolees in breach of their licence could be recalled and have their licences revoked, with those recalled as a result of having committed an imprisonable offence being ineligible for recall for 12 months or until a third of the period during which the licence would have remained in force had elapsed, whichever was the longer.

Throughcare is defined by SWSG as "the term used to denote the provision of a range of social work services to prisoners and their families, from the point of custodial remand or sentence, during the period of imprisonment and following release back into the community" (SWSG, 1993, para. 5.1). The aim of throughcare services, whether provided on a voluntary or compulsory basis is, according to Paragraph 5.6 of the Summary of National Objectives and Standards (SWSG, 1993):

"...to assist prisoners and ex-prisoners to address their offending and to help them to re-settle into law-abiding lives in the community. In the case of persons subject to statutory supervision on release the local authority is also responsible for supervising their compliance with the licence conditions and for taking action to advise the appropriate authorities of non-compliance. Throughcare services may also be provided, by the local authority and the independent sector, to the families of serving or discharged prisoners, to help them deal with problems generated by the family member's imprisonment, and to help the family adjust to the changed circumstances arising from the person's absence and eventual return to the community."

The throughcare process has three distinct stages. The first stage relates to the point of sentence when all offenders who receive a custodial remand or sentence should be interviewed by the court social worker to identify any immediate practical problems, to provide the prisoner with information about prison social work services and to assess whether the person may be at risk of self-injury and advise the prison authorities accordingly.

The second stage of throughcare relates to the period of imprisonment. Local authority social work departments provide a prison social work service in every penal establishment in Scotland. The task for prison social workers is described by SWSG (1993, para. 5.9) as being:

"...to try to motivate prisoners to examine their offending and, where possible, to assist them to tackle this behaviour through the provision of appropriate programmes and opportunities, in conjunction with the Scottish Prison Service, other specialists in the prison, and colleagues in the community."

The majority of work with serving prisoners will be undertaken by prison based social workers, though community based social workers may be involved in targeted work with prisoners and will, in the main, be responsible for undertaking longer term work with prisoners' families. In the later stages of the sentence, however, the balance will shift towards an increased level of contact between community based social workers and prisoners who will be in receipt of statutory supervision or voluntary assistance on release. In the case of prisoners who will be subject to statutory supervision, the prison social worker should be instrumental in bringing together the two strands of pre-release work by convening a meeting between the prisoner, the prison and community based social workers and any other interested parties at least one month prior to the prisoner's release. The purpose of the pre-release meeting is to "refine the prisoner's pre- and post-release plans, to agree the allocation of tasks between all concerned, and to indicate the likely level of contact with the supervisor for the first three months after release" (SWSG, 1993, para. 5.13).

The final stage of throughcare relates to the period following the release of the prisoner and involves the provision of services or advice to ex-prisoners either on request or combined with supervision as a condition of release on licence. Supervising social workers are required to determine the level and intensity of contact with regard to such factors as the assessed risk of re-offending and the expectations of the Parole Board and the Secretary of State, and with reference to the guidance contained in the National Standards, and to undertake formal reviews of the progress of supervision at regular intervals. Supervising social workers are, in addition, required to notify the relevant authorities of any conviction for a further offence or of other failure on the part of the ex-prisoner to comply with the terms of the licence.

The National Standards for throughcare services (SWSG, 1991, paras. 8.1-9.4) identify the primary objectives of statutory supervision as being:

- to assist offenders to reduce the risk of their re-offending;

- to seek to ensure that offenders released on statutory supervision adhere to their licence conditions;

- to facilitate the early release of prisoners who are eligible for statutory supervision; and

- to assist ex-prisoners to re-integrate successfully into the community.

The secondary objectives of statutory supervision are:

- to seek to limit and redress the damaging consequences of imprisonment for prisoners and their families, including the dislocation of family and community ties, the loss of personal choice, and the resultant stigma;

- to assist the families of prisoners to cope and to deal with the practical and emotional consequences of a member's offending and imprisonment;

- to help prisoners and their families to develop their ability to tackle their own problems; and

- to assist the families of ex-prisoners to adjust to the changed circumstances arising from the prisoner's return.

The objectives of voluntary support, on the other hand (SWSG, 1991, paras. 11.1-7), are:

- to provide and facilitate a range of services for prisoners and ex-prisoners and, where appropriate, their families, to assist them to deal with any problems they may face particularly following release;

- to assist offenders to reduce the risk of their re-offending through the provision of a range of services to meet identified needs;

- to seek to limit and redress the damaging consequences of imprisonment including the dislocation of family and community ties, the loss of personal choice, and the resultant stigma;

- to help prisoners and their families to develop their ability to tackle their own problems;

- to help prisoners and their families, on request, to prepare for release;

- to assist the families of released prisoners to adjust to the changed circumstances arising from the prisoner's return, where such a service is needed and requested; and

- to assist ex-prisoners to re-integrate successfully into the community and thus reduce the incidence of crime.

In defining the operational principles for throughcare the National Standards (SWSG, 1991, para. 12) recognise that:

> "It is not possible to say with any certainty that a throughcare programme or voluntary support on release will have a specific effect on re-offending; it is also virtually impossible to separate the effects of supervision or support from the many other factors which may impinge on an individual and contribute to behavioural change. However, many prisoners have problems with unemployment, homelessness, unstable domestic life, misuse of alcohol or drugs and long standing previous offending. Social work intervention must address these problems if it is to have any chance of meeting its objectives."

As such, the National Standards (SWSG, 1991, paras. 13.1-6) require that services to serving and discharged prisoners must:

- have as their central focus those factors which may precipitate offending behaviour, and the acquisition of new skills, attitudes or behaviours which will help offenders to reduce their offending;

- engage the offender in an agreed action plan which sets out the contribution the social worker, the offender and others will make to tackle problem behaviour, and to address personal and domestic needs;

- recognise, address, and seek to resolve or ameliorate, the pressing financial problems which many ex-prisoners face on release, and which may adversely affect their chances of effective resettlement;

- provide access to advice and help with personal, social, financial and family problems, especially those which may impede resettlement into the community;

- in the case of statutory supervision, state explicitly the supervisor's and offender's obligations and the way in which the conditions of the order will be enforced; and

- in the case of statutory supervision, ensure that any apparent breach of licence conditions is followed up rapidly by the supervising officer.

The National Standards provide a framework for throughcare services by setting benchmarks which should "promote and encourage the development and application of professional skills in management and practice" (SWSG, 1991, para. 5). The standards relate to each of the three stages of throughcare previously described and provide detailed guidance on the role of criminal justice social work services in respect of contact with the prisoner immediately following sentence; the preparation of reports; pre-release work; voluntary assistance; supervision in the community (including the level and intensity of supervision, formal review of progress and methods and models of supervision); and the enforcement and transfer of licences.

At the time of writing the National Standards for throughcare were undergoing revision to enable them to reflect changes in arrangements for the release of prisoners contained in the Prisoners and Criminal Proceedings (Scotland) Act 1993. Provisions contained in the Act came into effect in October 1993. They included the discontinuation of mandatory aftercare for young offenders and the introduction of a new measure - the supervised release order - which can be imposed by the courts upon offenders sentenced to periods of imprisonment of between 12 months and four years whom the courts believe could pose a risk of serious harm on release, requiring that the offender be subject to mandatory supervision for up to 12 months following release.

The Act also removed the option of parole for prisoners serving sentences of up to four years. Instead, such short term prisoners will be released unconditionally (unless subject to a supervised release order) after serving half their sentence. However, further conviction for an imprisonable offence during the unexpired portion of the sentence could result in any prisoner being recalled to prison by the court for any period until the date on which the original sentence would have expired in full.

Prisoners serving determinate sentences of four years or more can, under the new provisions, be released on parole licence after having served half their sentence and, if parole was not applied for or not granted, will be released on mandatory licence after serving two-thirds of the sentence originally passed. Prisoners released under either arrangement will be on licence until the date of expiry of the full sentence, during which time they can be recalled for non-compliance to serve up to the unexpired portion of the sentence.

Whilst the possible implications of the Prisoners and Criminal Proceedings (Scotland) Act 1993 will be discussed in the final chapter of this report, the present report focuses upon the statutory supervision of prisoners in the context of the arrangements which were in place when the National Standards for throughcare services were introduced and the framework of supervision and assistance which these standards provide.

METHODOLOGY

In three of the four study authorities, throughcare cases for inclusion in the sample were drawn from across the region as a whole. This step was taken to maximise the number of cases which could be identified within a given period of time. In the fourth area the focus was upon throughcare cases dealt with by two area teams in the district, including those held by a dedicated throughcare project (funded by the Urban Renewal Unit) which offered a service to offenders from areas of priority treatment (APTs) across the district.

In Burns social work services to the criminal justice system were delivered by specialist teams. Specialist arrangements existed to middle management level for the strategic and operational management of criminal justice services, with this area of work being located at senior management level within the adult assessment section of the department which also included community care. In Bruce criminal justice social work services were delivered by specialist teams with generic management arrangements above the level of team manager. As in Scott, operational management and strategic planning and co-ordination functions had been separated. In Bruce, however, responsibility for the latter was centralised. In Scott services were delivered by practitioners in split posts, each of whom devoted a percentage of their time to offender services and the remainder to generic social work tasks. Above the level of senior social worker, generic management arrangements prevailed. Planning and co-ordination functions were, however, devolved to a specialist co-ordinator at the local level. The dedicated throughcare project previously discussed was located in Scott. The greatest degree of specialisation was found in Wallace which had introduced specialist arrangements for service delivery and management to senior management level. With the exception of Scott, which was a predominantly urban area, the other three research sites, having a regional rather than local focus for the purposes of the throughcare study, contained a mixture of rural areas and urban centres of varying sizes.

The total possible sample consisted of all throughcare cases (parole, statutory aftercare and voluntary aftercare) which closed between 1 July 1994 and 30 April 1995 and which related to prisoners who had been released from custody since April 1992 (when the National Standards for throughcare came into effect). Also included were life licencees who, though still subject to statutory supervision, had been released from custody since April 1992.

Supervising social workers in each of the four research areas identified cases for inclusion in the study and sought the ex-prisoner's agreement a) to allow the researchers access to his/her social work file and b) to being interviewed about their experiences of community based throughcare. Such agreement was sought towards the end of the period of throughcare contact or, in the case of life licencees, at an appropriate point during the fieldwork period.

The participating social work departments adopted different approaches to recruit ex-prisoners into the sample. In Bruce and Scott, consent forms were issued in person, in the main, by the supervising social worker at the last point of contact with the ex-prisoner. In Wallace, covering letters and consent forms were sent to ex-prisoners shortly after case closure. An "opt-out" policy was adopted such that ex-prisoners who did not actively withhold their consent were assumed de facto to have agreed to participate in the research. In Burns, some ex-prisoners were issued with consent forms in person by their social workers. Delays in implementing the consent forms, however, meant that most ex-prisoners were sent consent forms by post. Burns insisted upon an "opt-in" policy with respect to research access such that ex-prisoners could be assumed to have consented to the researchers having access to their files only if they explicitly indicated this to be the case. As such, the sample size in Burns was significantly smaller than in the other three areas to the extent that less reliable conclusions could be drawn about the process or effectiveness of throughcare in that area.

The fieldwork for the research was completed between August 1994 and June 1995. The researchers visited each of the research sites on a regular basis to extract information from the case files of ex-prisoners who had agreed to participate in the study. Information relating to the characteristics of individual ex-prisoners and the process and outcomes of community based throughcare services was gathered from case files on pre-coded forms. The types of information collected are presented in Annex I.

Access was also obtained to prison social work files which are held centrally by the Scottish Prison Service following a prisoner's release. Such files generally contained little information above that which was recorded in the community based social work file and could not always be accessed with ease. If, for example, prisoners had been subject to very short periods of supervision the files may have still been located in the institutions from which they were released. If ex-prisoners had subsequently been recalled or had received a further custodial sentence, the prison social work file would have been forwarded to the receiving institution. More generally, information about the process of throughcare was derived from prison and community based social work files, and its accuracy is, therefore, dependent upon the comprehensive and accurate recording of that process in files.

After the relevant information had been extracted from case files, the social worker responsible for the case was issued a questionnaire to be completed in respect of the ex-prisoner. The questionnaire, which included a series of fixed choice and open-ended questions, sought to elicit information about the effectiveness of throughcare services in individual cases. The types of information sought in these questionnaires are listed in Annex II.

At the same time, all ex-prisoners whose case files had been examined were, unless they had explicitly expressed their unwillingness to be interviewed, contacted by letter to arrange an interview in their home. The purpose of the interviews was to explore ex-prisoners' experiences and perceptions of community based throughcare. The interviews, which lasted, on average, between one and one and a half hours, were semi-structured. The issues covered in the interviews are presented in Annex III.

The total sample consisted of 60 ex-prisoners who were subject to a variety of throughcare arrangements. Completed social workers' questionnaires were returned in respect of 48 of the sample and 31 ex-prisoners who had been subject to community based throughcare were interviewed. Fourteen of the ex-prisoners whose files had been examined agreed to be interviewed but failed to keep appointments with the researcher. Fifteen others had agreed to the researchers having access to their files but were unwilling to be interviewed, usually because they did not want to discuss their offences or wished, more generally, to put their experience of imprisonment or detention behind them.

Similar reasons were advanced by social workers for the refusal on the part of 11 ex-prisoners to agree to research access to their files and participation in the study. On the basis of brief anonymised information provided by social workers on pre-coded forms in the event of the ex-prisoner's refusal (which included gender, age, length of sentence served, main offence, type of throughcare, length of supervision period and reason for termination of contact) there was no evidence that prisoners who refused access differed in any marked respect from those who allowed the researchers access to their files. Nor did ex-prisoners who refused to be interviewed differ in any obvious respect from the total sample of which they were a part. Finally, the cases in which social workers completed questionnaires appeared to be largely similar to the sample as a whole. Therefore unless social workers exercised some discretion in respect of the cases identified for inclusion on the study, it can be assumed that the findings presented in this report are, in general, representative of throughcare practice in the participating study areas.

Interviews were conducted with social work managers, with social workers and with independent sector services providers in each of the four areas in the context of other studies within the present research programme. Where relevant, information derived from these interviews has been drawn upon in the present report to address the research questions previously outlined in this chapter.

CHAPTER TWO

EX-PRISONERS IN RECEIPT OF COMMUNITY BASED THROUGHCARE

INTRODUCTION

The present chapter describes the nature of throughcare arrangements which applied to the 60 ex-prisoners who formed the research sample and the characteristics of the sample. The cases were drawn from the four research areas and consisted of five in Burns, 23 in Bruce, 12 in Scott and 20 in Wallace. Where possible, cross-area comparisons will be drawn. However, the small number of cases in Burns often precludes meaningful comparisons of cases in this area with those in the other three research sites.

THE NATURE OF THROUGHCARE

The sample consisted of 35 parolees, eight other parolees subject to life licences, four young offenders in receipt of statutory aftercare, one ex-prisoner on a supervised release order and 12 ex-prisoners in receipt of voluntary assistance following release from custody.

Twenty-two of the 35 parolees and two life licencees had one or more additional requirements attached to their licences. Nine parolees were required to receive alcohol counselling and ten counselling regarding the use of drugs. Six ex-prisoners had been released with a requirement that they reside in a supported accommodation unit, three were required to obtain counselling/treatment regarding sexual offending and one was required to obtain help in controlling his temper. In total, then, more than half of the parole and life licences contained additional requirements attached by the Parole Board.

Three of the five ex-prisoners in Burns had been in receipt of voluntary assistance, one was a life licencee and one was subject to parole with a requirement to obtain alcohol counselling. Excluding the one supervised release order (in Wallace) the types of throughcare in each of the other three areas are summarised in Table 2.1.

Table 2.1: Type of throughcare by area[3]

	Bruce	Scott	Wallace	Total
Parole	5	4	4	13
Parole with additional requirements	11	3	7	21
Life licence	4	-	3	7
Statutory aftercare	1	2	1	4
Voluntary assistance	2	3	4	9
Total	23	12	19	54

There was relatively little difference in the type of throughcare by area, despite the existence in Scott of a dedicated throughcare project which offered a voluntary service to ex-prisoners on release from custody. Much of the work of this project, it would appear, was devoted to maintaining links with prisoners while they were in custody, with little evidence, during the fieldwork period at least, of any significant take-up of voluntary assistance on release. Just over half the parolees who had additional conditions in their licences were located in Bruce. This may be attributable to the existence of a range of supported accommodation provision in Bruce. Indeed, five of the six residential requirements pertained to ex-prisoners who were subject to supervision by social workers in that authority. Otherwise, it is not possible, in view of the relatively small number of cases with additional requirements, to comment upon whether the nature of additional requirements was influenced significantly by the availability of specialist resources in the four study areas. It is worth noting, however, that the only condition which required attendance at a sex offender intervention programme (as opposed to

---

[3] Excludes five cases in Burns and SRO in Wallace.

seeking counselling in relation to sexual offending) applied to an ex-prisoner in the only area (Wallace) in which provision of this type was available.

Three of the four young offenders subject to statutory aftercare were on licence for a period of 12 months and one was on a six month aftercare licence. The single supervised release order in the sample was for six months. The average period of supervision for the 48 offenders subject to some form of statutory supervision was 8.5 months. The average length of parole licences without additional requirements was 9.8 months and with additional requirements was 7.6 months. As Table 2.2 illustrates, the majority of parole licences, with or without additional requirements, were for periods of between six and 12 months. Ten parolees, were, however, subject to shorter periods of supervision (in 9 cases for 4 months or less) while four were on licence for longer periods of up to 18 months.

Table 2.2: Length of parole licence

	Without additional requirements	With additional requirements	Total
Less than 6 months	3	7	10
6-12 months	8	13	21
More than 12 months	2	2	4
Total	13	22	35

In Burns there was only one non-life parole licence which was for a duration of eight months. The average period of parole supervision was highest in Scott (12.0 months) and lowest in Bruce (6.2 months). In Wallace parolees were subject to supervision, on average, for a period of 8.6 months following release.

The offences for which offenders had received their sentences of imprisonment or detention are summarised in Table 2.3. Forty-two per cent of the sample had been sentenced for non-sexual crimes of violence, including serious assault, assault with intend to rob, robbery and murder. Twenty-five per cent had been sentenced for the possession (6 cases), supply (8 cases) or importing (1 case) of Class A or Class B drugs. Eight of the ten additional requirements to obtain drug counselling on release pertained to ex-prisoners convicted of drug offences.

Table 2.3: Main offence resulting in custodial sentence

	Number of cases	Percentage of cases
Non-sexual crimes of violence	25	42%
Drugs	15	25%
Dishonesty	9	15%
Sexual	7	12%
Fire-raising	2	3%
Firearms	1	2%
No information	1	2%

The type of offence in respect of which the custodial sentence had been imposed differed slightly by area. Three of the five ex-prisoners in Burns had been sentenced for offences involving dishonesty, one had been sentenced for murder and one for rape. The pattern of offences across the other three areas is summarised in Table 2.4. It should be noted that, because of the relatively small numbers of sexual offences, offences involving dishonesty, fire-raising and the possession of firearms, these categories have been grouped together in the "other" category in Table 2.4.

Table 2.4: Main offence by area[4]

	Bruce	Scott	Wallace	Total
Non-sexual crimes of violence	8	8	8	24
Drugs	6	2	7	15
Other	9	1	5	15
Total	23	11	20	54

---

[4] Information missing in one case.

Most ex-prisoners in Scott had been sentenced for non-sexual crimes of violence. Offenders in Bruce and Wallace, on the other hand, were more likely than those in Scott to have been imprisoned for offences involving drugs.

Only seven offenders had been imprisoned for an offence carrying a gravity rating[5] of less than three. Twenty-eight custodial sentences had been for main offences with a gravity rating of three, five for offences with a gravity rating of four and 19 for offences with a maximum gravity rating of five. The average gravity rating was similar across the four study areas (3.4 in Burns, 3.7 in Bruce, 3.3 in Scott and 3.7 in Wallace). Nor did the average gravity ratings of the original offences differ between offenders subject to parole licences with or without additional requirements and those in receipt of voluntary assistance on release (3.6, 3.3 and 3.1 respectively).

Around a third of the sample (21 offenders) had received their custodial sentence for a single offence (including 7 of the 8 ex-prisoners who had been sentenced to life imprisonment for murder). Fourteen offenders had been sentenced for two offences, 18 for three or four offences and six for five or more. In one case the number of offences in respect of which the offender had been sentenced was unknown. Offenders sentenced for non-sexual crimes of violence or for drug offences as the main offence were more likely than those sentenced for other types of offences to have received their prison sentence for a single offence (48 per cent and 38 per cent respectively). Ex-prisoners who had received a custodial sentence for sexual offences or for offences involving dishonesty, on the other hand, were more likely to have been convicted of three or more offences when the sentence of detention or imprisonment was imposed (57 per cent and 67 per cent respectively).

The length of custodial sentence imposed varied, in the case of determinate sentences, from two months to 12 years. Twelve ex-prisoners had been sentenced to periods of imprisonment or detention of up to two years; 33 had served sentences of between two and five years; and six had been imprisoned for periods in excess of five years. In one case the length of sentenced served was unknown. The average sentence length was 40 months. The average length of sentence imposed was lower for offences involving dishonesty than for the other categories of main offence (21.3 months compared with 46.2 for non-sexual crimes of violence, 51.4 for sexual offences and 41.5 for offences involving the possession, supply or importation of drugs). Ex-prisoners who had been sentenced for offences carrying a gravity rating of between one and three had received shorter determinate sentences, on average, than those sentenced for more serious offences carrying a gravity rating of four or five (35.7 months compared with 52.4 months).

The shortest average determinate prison sentences (18.5 months) had been served by ex-prisoners in Burns, three of whom had been in receipt of voluntary assistance on release. Otherwise, offenders in Bruce, Scott and Wallace had been sentenced to custody, on average, for similar periods of time (43.6 months, 43.3 months and 40.0 months respectively). Ex-prisoners whose throughcare contact had been on a voluntary basis had served, on average, shorter sentences than those subject to parole with or without additional requirements (18.7 months, 53.0 months and 50.6 months respectively).

THE CHARACTERISTICS OF EX-PRISONERS IN RECEIPT OF THROUGHCARE

With the exception of two women who had been offered voluntary assistance on release from custody, the other ex-prisoners in the sample were male. Only eight offenders (all male) were under 21 years of age when released from custody. Four of this group were subject to statutory aftercare, two were on parole, one was in receipt of voluntary assistance and one was subject to a Supervised Release Order(SRO). Five young offenders had been sentenced for non-sexual crimes of violence, one for offences involving dishonesty and one for offences related to the misuse of drugs. The nature of the main offence in the other case was unknown. Four of the young offenders were in Scott, where they accounted for a third of the 12 aftercare cases in that area. The average age of ex-prisoners in Scott (25.6 years) was slightly lower than that in Burns, Bruce and Wallace (29.8, 33.3 and 34.6 years respectively).

The average age of ex-prisoners in the sample as a whole was 31.9 years. Life licencees (whose average age was 43.1 years when released) were older, on average, than adult ex-prisoners in receipt of voluntary assistance (32.7 years) or subject to parole (30.8 years). Three life licencees were between 30 and 39 years of age when released and five were 40 years of age or older. The ages of the sample by type of throughcare are summarised in Table 2.5.

---

[5] The gravity rating employed by Creamer et al. (1993) in the calculation of a risk of custody score was employed. This assigns offences a gravity rating of one to five, with the least serious offences being assigned a gravity rating of one and the most serious a gravity rating of five.

Table 2.5[6]: Age by type of throughcare

	Voluntary	Statutory aftercare	Parole	Life licence	Total
16-20	1	4	2	-	7
21-30	5	-	16	-	21
31-40	3	-	11	3	17
41 and over	3	-	6	5	14
Total	12	4	35	8	59

The marital status of offenders on their release from custody was known in 58 cases. Half (29) were single, a third (19) were married or cohabiting and around a sixth (10) were separated, divorced or widowed.

Half the sample either returned to the parental home (17) or to their own or shared tenancies (13) following their release. Ten ex-prisoners were living with other relatives (6) or with friends (4), five were in private rented accommodation, three were owner occupiers and one was in a hostel. Nine ex-prisoners were resident in supported accommodation (8 in Bruce and one in Wallace) and in two cases the type of accommodation to which offenders returned was unknown.

Just over half the sample (31) had no dependent children. Fourteen had dependent children living in the same household and 13 had children living elsewhere. Information about the existence or otherwise of dependent children was unavailable in two cases.

Four-fifths of the ex-prisoners in receipt of throughcare (48) were unemployed when they returned to the community and only seven were in employment. Two were described as not seeking work, one was on a government training scheme and information about employment status was unavailable in two cases.

Table 2.6: Previous criminal history

	Previous convictions	Previous custodial sentences
Nil	11	25
One to Five	22	25
Six to Ten	10	5
Eleven or more	15	3
No information	2	2
Total	60	60

The criminal histories of the sample are summarised in Table 2.6. The majority of ex-prisoners had one or more previous convictions when sentenced to detention or imprisonment and a quarter had 11 or more. Just over half had previously served a custodial sentence. The average number of previous convictions and previous custodial sentences was highest in Burns (16.5 and 7.8 respectively) though the number of offenders involved (4) was small. Three of these ex-prisoners were previously known to the social work department and had been contacted in prison with an offer of voluntary assistance on release. Ex-prisoners in Bruce had slightly fewer previous convictions, on average, than did those in Scott and Wallace (5.1 compared with 7.8 and 7.4) and the former had served, on average, fewer previous custodial sentences (1.5 compared with 2.0 in Scott and 2.2 in Wallace). This may be a result of the availability of supported accommodation in Bruce and its take-up by ex-prisoners with less serious criminal histories who had been sentenced for more serious offences.

Ex-prisoners who were in receipt of voluntary assistance on release had more previous convictions, on average, than did those who were subject to statutory supervision (11.1 compared with 6.2) and the former group had served, on average, more previous custodial sentences (4.3 compared with 1.7). This may reflect a higher incidence of persistent offending, though of a less serious nature, among the voluntary throughcare sample. Some of those eligible for statutory throughcare, on the other hand, may have been imprisoned for a longer period of time for more serious, though relatively isolated, offences.

Finally, 18 throughcare clients were known to have been subject to supervision through the children's hearing system, 13 of whom had been subject to residential supervision requirements. Twenty-four ex-prisoners had previously received community based social work disposals: nine had been on probation; seven had undertaken community service; and eight had been sentenced to both probation and community service at previous court appearances.

---

[6] Excludes one young offender subject to an SRO.

SUMMARY

More than two-thirds of the sample of 60 ex-prisoners in receipt of community based throughcare were subject to parole and just over half of this group had additional requirements attached to their licences by the Parole Board. Additional requirements most frequently related to drug or alcohol counselling, residence and treatment for sexual offending. Most of the additional requirements in respect of drug counselling pertained to offenders who had been sentenced for offences involving drugs. Parolees in Bruce were most likely to have additional requirements attached to their licences.

Most parole licences were for durations of up to 12 months. The average period on licence was highest in Scott and lowest in Bruce. Just over two-fifths of the sample had been sentenced for non-sexual crimes of violence and a quarter for offences relating to the possession, supply or importation of drugs. Ex-prisoners in Bruce and Wallace were more likely to have been imprisoned for drug offences.

The majority of offences for which prisoners had received a custodial sentence carried a gravity rating of three or more. Around a third of the sample had been imprisoned for a single offence. The average length of determinate sentence imposed was 40 months. Ex-prisoners in receipt of voluntary assistance on release had served, on average, shorter sentences than those subject to statutory supervision.

The majority of the sample were males over 20 years of age. Life licencees were older, on average, than other groups of former prisoners. Half the sample were single and a similar proportion had returned to the parental home or to their own tenancy on release. Just under half had dependent children and the majority were unemployed on their return to the community.

The majority of ex-prisoners had one or more previous convictions and just over half had previously served a custodial sentence. Just under a third of prisoners in receipt of community based throughcare had been subject to supervision through the children's hearing system and more than a third had previous experience of community based social work disposals. Ex-prisoners in receipt of voluntary assistance had more extensive criminal histories, on average, than did those who were subject to statutory supervision on release.

CHAPTER THREE

THE PROCESS AND OUTCOMES OF COMMUNITY BASED THROUGHCARE

INTRODUCTION

The previous chapter examined the characteristics of ex-prisoners who were subject to community based throughcare in the four study areas. The present chapter focuses upon the process of throughcare with regard to issues such as the timing and frequency of contacts with the ex-prisoner, the types of services provided and nature of service provision and the outcomes of throughcare supervision in the community. In some instances the number of offenders in particular areas was relatively small or the numbers subject to different forms of throughcare were small. The majority of the analysis will, therefore, focus mainly upon the sample as a whole. Where relevant, however, the process of throughcare will be compared across areas and by the types of throughcare arrangements in force.

CONTACT WITH EX-PRISONERS SUBJECT TO THROUGHCARE

The National Standards for throughcare specify the type, timing, location and frequency of contacts which supervising social workers should have with prisoners subject to statutory supervision both prior to release and following their return to the community. The present section examines the frequency and nature of contact with ex-prisoners while in custody and during their period of community based throughcare.

Contact prior to release

The National Standards require that, in the case of prisoners who will be subject to parole or statutory after-care on release from custody, prison social workers should convene a three-way meeting between the prison-based social worker, the social worker who will be responsible for the community based element of throughcare and the prisoner. The purpose of such meetings is to "refine the prisoner's pre-and post-release plans, to agree the allocation of tasks and to indicate the likely level of contact with the supervisor during the first three months after release" (SWSG, 1991, para. 55).

Twenty-nine of the sample had, according to case records, been visited by their social worker in prison prior to release. One ex-prisoner in Burns, 11 each in Bruce and Wallace and six in Scott had received a pre-release visit. Such visits took place, on average, 45 days prior to the prisoner's release, though prisoners in receipt of voluntary aftercare were, on average, visited by their community based social workers at an earlier point in their sentences. Three young offenders subject to statutory after care, five ex-prisoners who received voluntary assistance, 18 parolees and three life licencees received a visit by their social worker while in custody. In some cases home leaves may have enabled social workers to establish contact with prospective parolees outwith the prison setting. In some other cases prison visits may have occurred which were not recorded in files which were "opened" on the date of the prisoner's release. In yet other cases it would appear that the short period of time between the Parole Board's decision to grant parole and the actual release date may have precluded a prison based meeting with the community based social worker responsible for the supervision of the parole licence (see also Chapter Five).

In 31 of the 48 statutory cases the community based social worker established contact with the prisoner's family while the prisoner was serving his/her sentence. In the majority of cases such contact was linked to the preparation of home circumstances reports for the Parole Board. In four cases support was provided to the families of prisoners on a voluntary basis. There was no indication in case files of contact being made with the families of 12 parolees, four life licencees and the ex-prisoner subject to a supervised release order. In some of these cases it is likely that such contact occurred but was not recorded in files. Some prisoners, however, did not have families to return to on release. Contact with prisoners' families took place, on average, around five months prior to the prisoner's release.

Contact following release

The National Standards specify that offenders subject to statutory throughcare should be seen within one working day of their release from custody. All but one ex-prisoners subject to statutory supervision were seen by their community based social worker within one week of their release (the remaining prisoner being seen eight days after being released from custody). The majority were seen on the day of release (25) or the following day (12). Both offenders in Burns, all nine in Scott, 71 per cent in Bruce and 69 per cent in Wallace were seen by their supervising social workers within one working day of their release from custody. Seventy-seven per cent of the overall sample were seen within the time-scale stipulated in the National Standards. Twenty-nine per cent of cases in Bruce and 31 per cent of those in Wallace did not meet the National Standard in this respect.

Ex-prisoners who are not subject to statutory supervision are eligible for voluntary assistance from the social work department during the 12 month period following their release from custody. The eight prisoners who received such voluntary assistance and for whom the relevant information was available first made contact with the social worker around six weeks (46 days) on average following their release from prison: one was seen on the day of release and two others within the first month. Two ex-prisoners sought assistance on a voluntary basis between one and two months following their return to the community and three between two and three months after their release.

In the case of ex-prisoners subject to statutory supervision in the community, the National Standards specify at least weekly contact in the first month and at least fortnightly contact throughout the remainder of the first three months. There should, therefore, be at least eight contacts with the ex-prisoner, at least one of which must be a home visit. Thereafter the level and intensity of supervision should be determined by the supervising social worker with regard to such factors as the risk of re-offending presented by the offender, the expectations of the Parole Board and Secretary of State, the framework of supervision, the outcome of formal reviews and the "assessed and changing needs for the provision of advice, guidance, assistance, and support for the offender and family" (SWSG, 1991, para. 71.5).

Information about the frequency of contact with ex-prisoners was available in respect of 46 offenders who were subject to statutory throughcare and who were in contact with the social work department for periods in excess of three months[7]. Only two cases in Burns fell into this category. As Table 3.1 indicates, the majority of interviews during this initial period of supervision took place with the offender alone. There was little difference in the average number of contacts across areas though social workers in Burns tended, on average, to see their clients slightly less frequently than did those in Scott or Wallace.

Table 3.1: Contact with ex-prisoners and their families in the first three months

	Ex-prisoner alone	With family	Total
Bruce (n=21)	6.6	0.2	6.8
Scott (n=8)	7.9	0.9	8.8
Wallace (n=15)	7.3	0.8	8.1

As Table 3.2 indicates, the majority of contacts with former prisoners were office based. The slightly higher total number of visits in Scott can, it appears, be attributable to a higher number of office based contacts in that area.

Table 3.2: Location of contacts during the first three months

	Office	Home	Total
Bruce (n=21)	4.7	2.1	6.8
Scott (n=8)	7.1	1.6	8.7
Wallace (n=15)	5.8	2.3	8.1

Neither of the two ex-prisoners in Burns were seen on eight or more occasions during the first three months. Standards were most often met in this respect in Scott where seven of the eight ex-prisoners were seen on eight or more occasions (in five cases nine or more contacts were made during this period). In Wallace, 60 per cent of offenders were seen at least eight times and all were seen on at least six occasions. In Bruce, however, only eight ex-prisoners (38 per cent) had levels of contact with their supervising social workers which met the National Standards and six others were seen on fewer than six occasions by their social workers during the initial three month period following release.

---

[7] One ex-prisoner who was subject to parole supervision for two months after release was not included since to do so would artificially lower the average number of contacts per case in the three months following release. In one other case accurate information about the frequency of contact could not be discerned from the case file.

Twenty-three of the 24 ex-prisoners who were still subject to supervision 12 months following release were seen, on average, on 8.6 occasions during the remainder of that first year (the relevant data were unavailable in one case). Thirteen were seen up to eight times during this period and ten were seen by their social workers on nine or more occasions. The relatively small numbers involved preclude any comparisons across areas.

Ex-prisoners who received voluntary assistance were seen on average on 4.9 occasions by their social worker. This compares with an average of 12.4 contacts with parolees and 13.2 with young offenders subject to statutory aftercare. The eight life licencees had been seen by their social worker, on average, 29.5 times at the point at which they agreed to participate in the study. Life licencees had, however, been subject to supervision for varying periods of time. One, for instance, had been released from custody in May 1992 while another had been in receipt of community based throughcare since January 1995. The lowest number of contacts recorded with a life licencee was seven while the highest was 89.

Reviews

The National Standards require that a formal review, involving the offender and, where relevant, the first line manager and/or other key individuals, should be held at the conclusion of the first three months of supervision. Subsequently formal reviews should be undertaken at 12 months and annually thereafter for the first five years of supervision. Further reviews beyond the first five years should be convened only as required. Since all of the prisoners in the present sample had been released from prison or young offenders institution since April 1992, none of the life licencees had been at liberty for more than three years when they agreed to participate in the study.

The purpose of the three monthly review is, according to the National Standards, to examine progress since release from prison, to identify continuing or new tasks and allocate responsibility for each task, and to determine the extent of contact until the next formal review. The 12 month review should set new objectives, targets and tasks for the next 12 months, while the annual reviews thereafter should, among their other tasks, determine the nature and form of supervision until the next review.

Formal reviews were held in a total of 29 cases. Fifteen ex-prisoners had one review, six had two reviews, six had three reviews and one each had four and five reviews. In total, therefore, 54 reviews were recorded as having occurred in these 29 cases. The majority of reviews recommended no change to the objectives of supervision. In two cases the objectives were amended following the first review and in a third case after a second review.

Initial reviews were conducted, on average, 17.1 weeks after the offender's release from custody. In Bruce reviews were conducted, on average, after 14.2 weeks. This compares with an average of 17.5 weeks in Scott and 19.0 weeks in Wallace. In 14 cases the initial review was conducted within 14 weeks of the ex-prisoner's release: just over half the reviews, therefore, (52 per cent) fell outwith the period stipulated in the National Standards. One of the two initial reviews in Burns, five out of nine in Bruce, three out of six in Scott and five out of 12 in Wallace were conducted within 14 weeks. Whilst the relatively small numbers of reviews in each study area limits the comparisons that can be drawn, there appeared to be no clear evidence of differential practice across social work authorities in this respect.

According to the National Standards, first line managers, while not required to attend all reviews, should do so if this is desirable in the interests of good case management or if requested to do so by the offender. Twenty-two of the 54 reviews were conducted with the senior social worker present. Five reviews, all in Bruce, were attended by the offender's keyworker from a supported accommodation unit and one was attended by a community service officer. As Table 3.3 illustrates, reviews in Scott were most likely to be attended by the senior social worker while this was least likely to be the case in Wallace. In Burns the senior social worker was present at three of the five recorded reviews. It is impossible to know what significance to attach to the senior social worker's absence from reviews. The policy adopted in Scott was that first line managers should normally attend reviews in the interests of good case management but the impact that this had upon the effectiveness of supervision and, therefore, the necessity of their presence at all reviews, is difficult to discern.

Table 3.3: Participants at reviews by area[8]

	Bruce	Scott	Wallace	Total
Social worker	4	1	20	25
Social worker and senior	3	11	4	18
Social worker and keyworker	5	-	-	5
Social worker, senior and CS officer	-	1	-	1
Total	12	13	24	49

8 Excludes five reviews in Burns.

SERVICES PROVIDED IN THE CONTEXT OF THROUGHCARE

The focus of the present research is primarily upon the services provided to ex-prisoners in receipt of throughcare by community based social workers. The present section examines the social worker's role prior to release and following the prisoner's return to the community.

Services provided prior to release

The National Standards define the period in prison as the second stage of the throughcare process (the first being contact with the prisoner at the point of remand or custodial sentence by court based social workers). Whilst prison based social workers will be responsible for most work undertaken with serving prisoners, social workers in the community may be involved in targeted work with prisoners and will normally undertake longer term work with prisoners' families. The Summary of National Objectives and Standards (SWSG, 1993, para. 5.10) suggests that "this balance will shift in the final stages of the sentence, towards an increased level of contact between workers in the community and those prisoners who will be in receipt of statutory supervision or voluntary assistance on release".

Table 3.4: Services provided prior to release

	By community based social worker (n=60)	By prison based social worker (n=60)
Accommodation	22	12
Employment	18	7
Relationships	15	8
Financial	14	7
Drugs	11	5
Offending	9	6
Alcohol	6	5
Use of leisure time	5	-
Education	4	-
Health	3	2
Violence	3	2
Social skills	1	1
Other	3[9]	4[10]

Table 3.4 summarises the services which were known, from community based and prison based social work files, to have been provided to prisoners in the sample prior to their release from custody. The list cannot be assumed to be exhaustive: in some instances prison social work files could not be traced and it is possible that other work was undertaken which had not been recorded in case files. It does, however, indicate the relative prominence of different issues prior to a prisoner's release.

Table 3.4 suggests that much of the work undertaken with prisoners at this stage was of an essentially practical nature, involving attention to issues which might assist in facilitating the prisoner's resettlement in the community on release. Accommodation, employment and financial matters predominated, although in a significant number of cases social workers focused upon family or personal relationships. The latter might, for example, involve liaising with the prisoner's family to prepare them for the prisoner's release and discussing with the prisoner the implications of returning to the community after what may have been a lengthy absence.

Service needs identified prior to and following release

Where contact between prisoners and community based social workers occurred while the prisoner was still serving his/her sentence, an opportunity would be afforded to identify potential areas of work on release. In

---

[9] Completion of community service order (2) requirements of licence (1).
[10] Requirements of licence (2) compassionate leave (1) access to children (1).

the absence of such contact prisoners' needs would, by necessity, be identified once they had returned to the community. Even in cases in which contact had been established at the pre-release stage, however, other issues may have emerged following the prisoner's release from custody.

Table 3.5 summarises those issues identified as requiring attention by community based social workers at the pre-release stage and following the prisoner's return to the community. In cases where different issues within the same broad heading were identified before and after release, these have not been recorded separately. The "after release" category, therefore, applies only to areas of work in which no issues had previously been identified within a particular heading and, as such, the column totals in Table 3.5 are mutually exclusive.

As with the pre-release work undertaken with serving prisoners, practical issues such as employment, financial matters and accommodation most often featured as areas requiring attention on release. Family or personal relationships also featured prominently in pre-release work with prisoners and were more likely than other issues to gain prominence once the prisoner had returned to the community.

Table 3.5: Service needs identified before and after release

	Prior to release	After release	Total (n=60)	
Employment	22	11	33	(55%)
Financial	17	15	32	(53%)
Accommodation	16	15	31	(52%)
Offending	16	12	28	(47%)
Relationships	13	18	31	(52%)
Alcohol	11	1	12	(20%)
Drugs	9	6	15	(25%)
Use of leisure time	4	7	11	(18%)
Education	3	4	7	(12%)
Violence	3	3	6	(10%)
Health[11]	3	3	6	(10%)
Social skills	1	3	4	(7%)
Other	-	4	4[12]	(7%)

The number of throughcare cases in each area was relatively small, preventing any firm conclusions to be reached with regard to area differences in the types of issues identified for inclusion in post-release packages. However, accommodation was more often identified in Scott (58 per cent of cases compared with 17 per cent in Bruce and 15 per cent in Wallace), as were financial problems (50 per cent compared with 26 per cent and 15 per cent), employment (50 per cent compared with 39 per cent and 30 per cent) and alcohol abuse (33 per cent compared with 20 per cent and 9 per cent). Drug abuse was most often identified as an issue in Wallace (25 per cent of cases compared with 9 per cent in Bruce and 17 per cent in Scott) as was addressing offending behaviour (40 per cent compared with 22 per cent and 17 per cent). Area differences in the frequency with which different issues were identified cannot be accounted for by differences in the types of throughcare arrangements which prevailed or by the proportion of ex-prisoners in each area who had been visited by their community based social worker prior to release.

Further analysis of the issues identified by community based social workers prior to release for inclusion in post-release packages revealed some interesting differences according to the age of the ex-prisoner and the type of throughcare arrangements which applied. Table 3.6 summarises the issues identified for post-release services for the 55 ex-prisoners who were in receipt of voluntary assistance or who were subject to parole supervision (including life licencees). Because the numbers of ex-prisoners subject to a supervised release order or statutory aftercare were small (5) these cases have been excluded from the analysis. So too have those issues which were identified in fewer than four cases.

The numbers of cases to which each type of throughcare applied were still relatively small, preventing any firm conclusions to be drawn from the results. The relative significance of different issues varied, however,

---

[11] Includes psychiatric problems.
[12] Effects of imprisonment (2) child care (1) completion of community service order (1).

according to the type of throughcare concerned. In the case of voluntary assistance, accommodation featured as the most salient issue, followed by financial matters, alcohol abuse and employment. Employment and relationships followed by offending featured most commonly among parolees who had no additional requirements attached to their licences. Among those who did have additional requirements attached, offending was the most frequently identified issue, followed by employment, alcohol and drugs. This pattern of findings is consistent with the earlier observation that the majority of additional requirements related to counselling for problems related to the misuse of alcohol or drugs. In the case of life licencees, essentially practical issues - financial matters, employment and accommodation - were most often identified as part of the post-release supervision package.

Table 3.6: Issues identified for post-release services by type of throughcare

	Voluntary (n=12)		Parole (n=13)		Parole with additional requirements (n=22)		Life licence (n=8)	
Accommodation	5	(42%)	3	(23%)	3	(14%)	3	(38%)
Alcohol	2	(17%)	-		6	(27%)	2	(25%)
Drugs	1	(8%)	1	(8%)	6	(27%)	-	
Employment	2	(17%)	6	(46%)	7	(32%)	5	(62%)
Financial	3	(25%)	3	(23%)	3	(14%)	6	(75%)
Use of leisure	-		-		2	(9%)	2	(25%)
Offending	1	(8%)	5	(38%)	8	(36%)	2	(25%)
Relationships	-		6	(46%)	4	(18%)	2	(25%)

Life licencees were more likely than other categories of ex-prisoner to have financial matters and employment identified at the pre-release stage for post-release work. There was also slightly less emphasis placed on offending behaviour in respect of life licencees in comparison with parolees. This is consistent with the study of Parole Board decision making (McAra, 1998) which suggested that risk of further offending tended to be a less important consideration for parole decision makers in the case of prisoners serving indeterminate as opposed to determinate sentences.

Turning now to the relationship between the nature of pre-release packages and age, the relevant data are presented in Table 3.7. Again, issues which pertained to a small number of cases (fewer than 4) have been excluded.

Table 3.7: Issues identified for post-release services by age

	16-25 years (n=22)		26 years and over (n=38)	
Accommodation	4	(18%)	12	(32%)
Alcohol	4	(18%)	7	(18%)
Drugs	5	(23%)	4	(10%)
Employment	8	(36%)	14	(36%)
Financial	7	(32%)	10	(26%)
Use of leisure	-		4	(10%)
Offending	3	(14%)	13	(34%)
Relationships	2	(9%)	11	(38%)

Employment, financial matters and drug use were the issues most commonly identified among ex-prisoners who were under 26 years of age when released. Employment, offending, accommodation and relationships featured most commonly (in that order) in the pre-release packages identified for older offenders. Drug use was the only issue identified significantly more often among the younger age group (though financial matters were also somewhat more likely to be identified for this group of ex-prisoners). By contrast, accommodation, offending and relationships (and, to a lesser extent, use of leisure time) featured more often in the pre-release plans for older ex-prisoners. The greater emphasis placed upon offending behaviour with older ex-prisoners cannot readily be explained by the available data. It cannot, for example, be attributed to a higher proportion of voluntary cases in the younger age group, nor did the two groups differ according to their previous criminal histories. It may, however, partly reflect differences in the types of offences for which the two age groups had been imprisoned. The younger offenders were more likely to have been imprisoned for non-sexual crimes of violence. On the other hand, all of the seven ex-prisoners who had been sentenced for sexual offences were over 25 years of age when released as were the eight life licencees. Offending was identified as an area for post-release services in respect of two life licencees and four sexual offenders. By contrast, it featured in only two of the 17 cases involving non-sexual crimes of violence other than murder.

The nature of services provided

The range of services provided by community based social workers following the prisoner's release from custody are summarised in Table 3.8. The relative frequency of different services is, by and large, consistent with the relative frequency with which different issues had been identified as requiring attention prior to or following release. As in the study of probation supervision which forms part of the present research programme, the majority of service provision or intervention was undertaken on a one-to-one basis. In comparison with probation, however, the offending itself was slightly less likely to feature in the work undertaken with ex-prisoners in receipt of throughcare.

3.8: Method of service provision

	Individual	Group	Both	Total (n=60)	
Accommodation	31	-	-	31	(52%)
Relationships	30	-	-	30	(50%)
Financial	27	-	-	27	(45%)
Offending	26	-	1	27	(45%)
Employment	23	3	1	27	(45%)
Drugs	14	-	-	14	(23%)
Use of leisure time	11	-	-	11	(18%)
Alcohol	10	1	-	11	(18%)
Education	6	-	-	6	(10%)
Violence	6	-	-	6	(10%)
Health	4	-	-	4	(7%)
Social skills	4	-	-	4	(7%)
Other	4	-	-	4	(7%)

As Table 3.9 illustrates, the majority of work with former prisoners was undertaken by social workers themselves. The only areas of work in which other agencies were involved to any significant extent related to employment and alcohol or drug abuse. Again this pattern of results is consistent with the findings of the probation study, which also revealed that supervising social workers were responsible, in the main, for work undertaken in relation to a wide spectrum of services.

The types of services provided to release prisoners appeared to vary by area, though the small number of cases prevent firm conclusions from being drawn. Social workers in Scott were more likely to focus upon accommodation (75 per cent of cases compared with 56 per cent in Bruce and 30 per cent in Wallace), employment (67 per cent compared with 35 per cent and 50 per cent) and financial issues (75 per cent compared with 35 per cent each in Bruce and Wallace). Social workers in Wallace more often focused upon offending behaviour (55 per cent of cases compared with 39 per cent in Bruce and 42 per cent in Scott) and the ex-prisoner's use of leisure time (30 per cent compared with 13 per cent and 9 per cent) and less often focused upon family or personal relationships (40 per cent compared with 56 per cent and 58 per cent). Finally, alcohol abuse featured slightly more often in services provided to ex-prisoners in Scott and Wallace (25 per cent and 20 per cent compared with 13 per cent in Bruce).

Table 3.9: Providers of services

	Social worker	Other agency	Social worker and other agency	Total (n=60)	
Accommodation	30	-	1	31	(52%)
Relationships	30	-	-	30	(50%)
Financial	26	-	1	27	(45%)
Offending	27	-	-	27	(45%)
Employment	19	6	2	27	(45%)
Drugs	10	4	-	14	(23%)
Use of leisure time	11	-	-	11	(18%)
Alcohol	2	7	2	11	(18%)
Education	6	-	-	6	(10%)
Violence	6	-	-	6	(10%)
Health	3	1	-	4	(7%)
Social skills	4	-	-	4	(7%)
Other	4	-	-	4	(7%)

There were relatively few differences in the types of services provided according to the age of the ex-prisoner, though drug abuse was more commonly a focus for intervention among ex-prisoners under 26 years of age (36 per cent compared with 16 per cent) while accommodation featured slightly more often among the services provided to ex-prisoners who were aged 26 years or older (55 per cent compared with 45 per cent).

The nature of services provided also differed to some extent according to the type of throughcare arrangements which applied. Accommodation, employment and financial issues each featured in work with three-quarters of the sample of life licencees. Accommodation was focused upon in 50 per cent of voluntary cases, 46 per cent of parole cases and 45 per cent of parole cases in which additional requirements were attached. Employment served as a focus for service provision in 25 per cent of voluntary cases, 69 per cent of parole cases and 36 per cent of parole cases with additional requirements. Financial issues were addressed in 33 per cent of voluntary cases, 46 per cent of parole cases and 36 per cent of parole cases with additional requirements. Offending featured more often in work with parolees who had additional requirements attached to their order (68 per cent compared with 38 per cent of parolees and life licencees and 17 per cent of voluntary cases) as did alcohol abuse (32 per cent compared with 17 per cent of voluntary cases, one life licensee and no parolees) and drug abuse (41 per cent compared with 25 per cent of voluntary cases, 15 per cent of parolees and no life licencees). The numbers of ex-prisoners in each category were small but the findings point to work with life licencees having been focused to a greater extent than with other groups of ex-prisoners upon practical issues associated with re-integration into the community. Services provided to parolees with additional requirements attached, on the other hand, both reflected the problems in relation to which additional requirements were imposed, and suggested that this group of prisoners was perceived by their supervising social workers as presenting a greater risk of continued offending behaviour than other ex-prisoners subject to statutory supervision on release. This particular issue will be explored further in the following chapter.

Fifty-two ex-prisoners had no change of social worker throughout their period on throughcare. All five offenders in Burns had a single social worker as did most of those in Bruce (96 per cent) and Wallace (85 per cent). Three of the 12 ex-prisoners in Scott had three social workers and a fourth had three. Staff changes and maternity leave accounted for the change of social worker in seven cases. In one other case the reason for the change was not recorded in the case file.

THE OUTCOMES OF SUPERVISION

The present section examines the outcomes of supervision with reference to the reasons for contact being terminated, ex-prisoners' compliance with statutory supervision, further offending during the period of throughcare and changes in the social circumstances of former prisoners since their release. First, however, the objectives of supervision and the extent to which they were deemed to have been achieved will be examined.

Objectives and their achievement

In each case included in the sample, an attempt was made by the researchers to identify up to four main objectives in the case and to assess, on a five point scale, the extent to which they had been achieved. In so doing, the researchers drew upon case notes, completion reports (where available), review reports and regular reports to the Parole Board in the case of life licencees. The present section, therefore, is based upon the researchers' views derived from a variety of sources rather than from any clear statement by the social worker of objectives set and progress made in individual cases.

In nine cases, no clear objectives could be identified from the social work case file. Table 3.10 summarises the main objectives identified from files and the extent to which they were considered to have been achieved. Other objectives which were identified in smaller numbers of cases were financial issues (4), get through the order (4), use of leisure time (3) peer group pressure (2) violence/aggression (2), improve self-esteem (1), support family (1), provide general support (1) and obtain driving licence (1).

The nature of objectives identified from case files varied to some extent by area. Thus employment was more often an objective in Scott (50 per cent of cases compared with 17 per cent in Bruce and 35 per cent in Wallace) as was accommodation (42 per cent compared with 17 per cent and 5 per cent). Resettling the offender in the community, as a general aim, featured more often in Bruce than in Wallace or Scott (30 per cent compared with 20 per cent and 25 per cent). Addressing offending, on the other hand, was more often an objective in Wallace than in the other two areas (35 per cent compared with 35 per cent in Scott and 17 per cent in Bruce).

Table 3.10: Objectives and their achievement

	Number of cases	Percentage of cases	Number achieved	Percentage achieved[13]
Employment	17	28%	11	65%
Resettle in the community	17	28%	13	76%
Offending	15	25%	14	93%
Accommodation	14	23%	9	64%
Drugs	10	17%	5	50%
Relationships	10	17%	5	50%
Alcohol	8	13%	6	75%

Addressing drug abuse was more often identified as an objective with ex-prisoners under 26 years of age (27 per cent compared with 10 per cent). Employment likewise tended to feature more often as an objective with younger offenders (36 per cent compared with 26 per cent) while resettling the ex-prisoner in the community was slightly more often identified as an objective with offenders aged 26 years or older (32 per cent compared with 23 per cent).

Accommodation featured more often as an objective in work with ex-prisoners who had requested voluntary assistance (42 per cent of cases compared with 15 per cent of parolees, 14 per cent of parolees with additional requirements and 25 per cent of life licencees). Employment was most often an objective with life licencees (50 per cent) and parolees (54 per cent) than with parolees who had additional requirements (23 per cent) and voluntary cases (8 per cent). Resettling the ex-prisoner in the community featured most often as an objective of work with life licencees (62 per cent compared with eight per cent of voluntary cases, 38 per cent of parolees and 27 per cent of parolees with additional requirements). Addressing alcohol abuse was more often an objective in work with parolees who had additional requirements (27 per cent compared with 17 per cent of voluntary cases, eight per cent of parolees and no life licencees) and this was also true of drug abuse (27 per cent compared with one voluntary case, no parolees and one life licencee). Again, therefore, although the numbers in each category are small, there is some evidence that throughcare services reflected the characteristics and needs of ex-prisoners subject to different throughcare arrangements.

Forty-eight per cent of objectives identified from case files were assessed as having been achieved in full, 28 per cent to a significant extent, 12 per cent partially and five per cent to a limited extent. No progress was considered to have been made in respect of only seven per cent of objectives set. As Table 3.8 illustrates,

---

[13] Percentage of objectives achieved completely or to a significant extent.

objectives related to preventing or addressing offending were considered in most cases to have been achieved in full or to a significant extent. Significant progress was also frequently made in relation to the broad objective of assisting the ex-prisoner to resettle in the community and in addressing alcohol abuse, although in respect of the latter the number of cases involved was small. Objectives relating to drug abuse and relationships were least often assessed as having been achieved completely or to a significant extent.

Objectives in Bruce were slightly less likely to have been achieved than those identified in work with ex-prisoners in Scott or Wallace (67 per cent compared with 85 per cent in the latter areas). Objectives identified in work with ex-prisoners under 26 years of age were as likely to have been achieved as those identified in work with older ex-prisoners (77 per cent compared with 75 per cent). Finally, objectives set in relation to ex-prisoners who had sought assistance on a voluntary basis were slightly less often achieved than those set with other categories of ex-prisoner (56 per cent compared with 73 per cent, 80 per cent and 70 per cent in the case of parolees with additional requirements and life licencees respectively).

Compliance and termination of contact

There was little evidence in case files of deliberate non-compliance with statutory requirements. Only two parolees received one formal warning for failure to report to the supervising officer and one received two. The Scottish Office Home and Health Department (now The Scottish Office Home Department) received notification in the latter case and agreed that supervision should continue. The parole licence was subsequently completed successfully.

Supervising social workers notified the Scottish Office in respect of further offending by three other parolees. Two, both of whom were reconvicted of offences involving dishonesty, were recalled to prison. In the third case, involving a conviction for criminal damage, supervision was allowed to continue. Overall, then, only two of the 48 ex-prisoners who were subject to statutory supervision on their release (both on parole licences without additional requirements) had been recalled to prison. None of the eight life licencees had been recalled or had received a formal warning since being released.

Six voluntary aftercare cases were terminated because social work support was no longer required. Four ex-prisoners' cases were closed after they ceased to maintain voluntary contact with the social work department. Voluntary assistance was terminated in one case when the offender received a further custodial sentence and one ex-prisoner, initially designated as eligible for voluntary aftercare and allocated to the criminal justice team, was re-allocated, on the basis of his drug use, to the community care team shortly after release.

Further offending

Eight ex-prisoners were subsequently convicted of a further offence committed while they were subject to community based throughcare and one other, who was on a parole licence with additional requirements, had been charged with further offending. Two ex-prisoners who were reconvicted had been in receipt of assistance on a voluntary basis and three (previously discussed) were on parole. Two young offenders on statutory aftercare licences were reconvicted but were neither recalled nor notified to the Scottish Office. The one offender who was made subject to a supervised release order was reconvicted but was not recalled to prison by the court. None of the eight life licencees had been reconvicted of, or charged with, a further offence.

Seven of this group of nine prisoners had been charged or convicted on one occasion and two had been reconvicted twice. In total, therefore, ten instances of further offending and one instance of alleged offending were recorded. Four convictions related to offences involving dishonesty, two were for assaults and one each were for serious assault, breach of the peace (sexual), criminal damage and breach of the peace. The outstanding charge, in respect of which the ex-prisoner whose case had still to come to court, involved theft.

Five convictions resulted in the offender receiving a custodial sentence. Two offenders were given deferred sentences, one was fined, one was given a compensation order and one was ordered to undertake community service.

Ex-prisoners who were reconvicted or charged with further offences had, on average, more previous convictions than those who had not re-offended while in receipt of community based throughcare (11.7 compared with 5.6). Ex-prisoners who were reconvicted or charged were, on average, younger than those who were not (21.8 years compared with 34.3 years). Four of those who were reconvicted were under 21 years of age. Indeed, half of the eight prisoners who were under 21 years of age when released from custody were reconvicted. By comparison, just under one in ten of those who were 21 years of age or over when released were reconvicted of or charged with a further offence.

The social circumstances of offenders on termination

One indicator of the success of community based throughcare relates to the relative social circumstances of ex-prisoners immediately following release and following their contact with the social work department. Two indices are of particular relevance here: employment status and housing circumstances.

As Table 3.11 indicates, almost half the sample had their own or shared tenancy following throughcare contact compared with less than a quarter immediately following release. In addition, fewer ex-prisoners were in temporary or potentially temporary living arrangements - supported accommodation units, hostels or living with relatives or friends - than was the case when their period of throughcare began.

Table 3.11: Accommodation on release and following throughcare contact

	On release	Following throughcare contact
Parental home	17 (28%)	12 (20%)
Own or shared tenancy	13 (22%)	29 (48%)
Supported accommodation	9 (15%)	3 (5%)
Other relatives	6 (10%)	3 (5%)
Private rented	5 (8%)	5 (8%)
Friends	4 (7%)	1 (2%)
Owner occupier	3 (5%)	2 (3%)
Hostel	1 (2%)	-
In custody	-	2 (3%)
No information	2 (3%)	3 (5%)
Total	60	60

The employment status of ex-prisoners is summarised in Table 3.12. Whilst the majority were still unemployed following throughcare contact, just over a third of the sample were employed, on government training schemes or in full-time education compared with fewer than one in seven immediately following their return to the community.

Table 3.12: Employment status on release and following throughcare contact

	On release	Following throughcare contact
Unemployed	48 (80%)	34 (57%)
Employed	7 (12%)	16 (27%)
Not seeking work	2 (3%)	3 (5%)
Government training scheme	1 (2%)	2 (3%)
Full-time education	-	3 (5%)
No information	2 (3%)	2 (3%)
Total	60	60

SUMMARY

Twenty-nine ex-prisoners had received a visit from their community based social worker while in custody and in 31 cases supervising social workers had established contact with prisoners' families, usually in connection with the preparation of a home circumstances report for the Parole Board. Most ex-prisoners on statutory supervision were seen by their supervising social worker within 24 hours of their release. Ex-prisoners who received voluntary assistance made contact, on average, six weeks after being released from custody.

Prisoners subject to statutory supervision had more contacts with their social workers than did those in receipt of voluntary assistance. Ex-prisoners in Scott had more office contacts with their social workers in the first three months of supervision and had slightly more contacts overall during this period than did those in the other areas. National Standards with respect to the frequency of contact in the first three months and the date of initial contact with statutory throughcare cases were more often met in Scott than in the other study areas.

Formal reviews were held in 29 cases with just over half of these former prisoners having a single review. Initial reviews were conducted, on average, 17 weeks after the prisoner's release. Few reviews resulted in amendments to the objectives of supervision. Senior social workers attended around two-fifths of reviews. Reviews in Scott were most likely to be attended by the social worker's first line manager and this was least likely to occur in Wallace.

The majority of services provided both at the pre-release stage and following release focused upon practical issues such as accommodation, financial matters and employment. The majority of work was undertaken on a one-to-one basis and, with the exception of employment services and services for offenders with problems related to the use of alcohol or drugs, most work was undertaken by the supervising social workers themselves. Objectives which were related to helping the ex-prisoner resettle in the community, offending behaviour and addressing alcohol abuse were most often achieved. Most ex-prisoners had the same social worker throughout their period of community based throughcare. Where a change of social worker occurred - and this was slightly more frequent in Scott - it was usually a result of staff absences or changes.

There were some variations in the services provided and objectives pursued across the study areas. Work in Scott, for example, more often focused on employment and accommodation, while the broader aim of re-settling the offender in the community was most prevalent in Bruce, and social workers in Wallace were most likely to focus upon offending behaviour. Resettling the ex-prisoner in the community was more often an objective with ex-prisoners aged 26 years or older while work with younger offenders was more likely to focus upon drug abuse.

Accommodation featured most often as an objective with voluntary cases. Work with life licencees was most clearly focused upon practical issues associated with the re-integration of the ex-prisoner in the community, while objectives pursued and services provided in respect of parolees with additional requirements most often focused upon offending behaviour, alcohol and drug abuse, suggesting that this category of ex-prisoner was perceived as presenting the greatest risk of further offending on release.

Few ex-prisoners received formal warnings while subject to supervision and only two were recalled to prison as a consequence of further offending: both, significantly in view of the previous argument, were parolees with additional requirements attached to their licences. Eight individuals were reconvicted of offences committed while in receipt of community based throughcare and one had been charged with an offence allegedly committed during this period. Young offenders were more likely than adults to have been reconvicted and those who were reconvicted had more serious offending histories as evidenced by the number of previous convictions and previous custodial sentences. Voluntary assistance was terminated in most instances because outstanding issues had been addressed or because the ex-prisoner ceased to maintain contact with the social work department.

There was some evidence of an improvement in ex-prisoners' social circumstances - as indicated by changes in living arrangements and employment status - following the period of community based throughcare.

CHAPTER FOUR

SOCIAL WORKERS' VIEWS OF THE EFFECTIVENESS OF COMMUNITY BASED THROUGHCARE

INTRODUCTION

Supervising social workers were invited, in respect of each of the cases included in the main study sample, to complete a brief questionnaire following the termination of the community based throughcare contact or, in the case of life licencees, at whatever point the post-release supervision had reached. The questionnaire, which consisted of a mixture of fixed choice and open ended questions, sought to elicit their views as to the effectiveness of community based throughcare in individual cases. Specific areas addressed in the questionnaire included the social worker's and ex-prisoner's definitions of the main issues in the case; objectives of supervision/voluntary assistance and the extent to which they were achieved; the ex-prisoner's response and what s/he found most and least helpful about throughcare; and social workers' perceptions of the risk of continued offending including, where relevant, the contribution of throughcare in reducing that risk. Forty-eight completed questionnaires were returned from a total possible sample of 60. The questionnaires related to eight young offenders aged between 16 and 20 years when released from custody and 40 adult ex-prisoners (aged 21 years and over). Nine offenders had been in receipt of voluntary assistance, 30 had been released on parole (with or without additional conditions), four were life licencees, four were subject to statutory aftercare and one was subject to a supervised release order. The relatively low numbers of young offenders and of offenders in receipt of voluntary assistance prevent any meaningful comparisons of findings by age and by basis of throughcare contact. The present chapter describes the findings from this element of the study.

SOCIAL WORKERS' AND EX-PRISONERS' DEFINITIONS OF ISSUES

Social workers were invited to identify what they perceived to have been the main issues in the case and what they believed the ex-prisoner had considered the main issues to have been. In both instances up to four separate issues could be identified in each case. Consistent with previous research (Duffee and Clark, 1985) social workers tended to identify more issues in a case than they considered that their clients did, though the difference was not marked (Table 4.1). For instance, while four main issues were defined by social workers in 28 cases, the same number of issues were believed by social workers to have been identified by only 20 ex-prisoners.

Table 4.1: Social workers' views as to the number of issues identified by them and by ex-prisoners

Number of issues	Social workers	Ex-prisoners
Four	28	20
Three	12	16
Two	4	10
One	4	2

The social workers' views of the main issues in each case and their perceptions of their clients' views are summarised in Table 4.2. It should be noted that in this, and in several other tables in this chapter, since more than one issue was identified in the majority of cases the column total exceeds the number of cases involved.

It is evident from Table 4.2 that there was broad agreement among social workers and their clients as to the main issues in the case. Social workers were, however, more likely to identify problematic drug or alcohol use and resettling in the community as issues requiring attention (alcohol problems were 8 per cent more likely to be identified by social workers and drug problems and resettling in the community 7 per cent more likely to be identified by them). Ex-prisoners were, on the other hand, more likely than social workers to attach significance to financial problems (17 per cent more likely) and employment/education (12 per cent more likely).

To the extent that ex-prisoners more readily identified immediate practical concerns, such as money and work, than did social workers, these findings are consistent with Duffee and Clark's (1985) review of studies which had sought to identify the needs of parolees and probationers in community settings.

Table 4.2: Social workers' perceptions of their and own and their clients' views of the main issues

Issue	Social workers' views	Ex-prisoners' views
Offending	24 (50%)	22 (46%)
Accommodation	23 (48%)	24 (50%)
Employment/education	22 (46%)	28 (58%)
Alcohol	12 (25%)	8 (17%)
Family relationships	11 (23%)	9 (19%)
Personal relationships	10 (21%)	10 (21%)
Drugs	9 (19%)	6 (12%)
Get through licence/avoid recall	8 (17%)	7 (15%)
Resettle in community	8 (17%)	5 (10%)
Emotional support	7 (15%)	6 (12%)
Financial	5 (10%)	13 (27%)
Use of leisure time	5 (10%)	3 (6%)
Aggression/violence	3 (6%)	1 (2%)
General/practical support	3 (6%)	3 (6%)
Child care	2 (4%)	0 (0%)
Monitor other conditions	2 (4%)	0 (0%)
Self-esteem	2 (4%)	0 (0%)
Attitudes supportive of offending	1 (2%)	1 (2%)
Peer group	1 (2%)	1 (2%)
Gambling	1 (2%)	1 (2%)
Support for family	1 (2%)	1 (2%)
Social/personal skills	1 (2%)	1 (2%)

THROUGHCARE OBJECTIVES AND THEIR ACHIEVEMENT

Social workers were asked, in each case, to identify up to four main objectives of throughcare and to indicate, on a five point scale, the extent to which they believed them to have been achieved. The relevant findings are summarised in Table 4.3. Overall, 29 per cent of objectives were assessed as having been achieved completely, 30 per cent to a significant extent, 23 per cent partially and 12 per cent to a limited extent. No progress was thought to have been made in respect of only six per cent of objectives. Success in achieving specific objectives was assessed in relation to the proportion of cases in which objectives were achieved totally or to a significant extent out of the total number of cases to which the objective applied. In some instances the number of cases in which a particular objective applied was small and firm conclusions can not, therefore, be drawn. It is still of interest, however, to examine the relative success with which different objectives were apparently achieved. Social workers, it appears, had greatest success in achieving objectives relating to alcohol use, addressing other practical issues, addressing other factors related to offending and helping ex-prisoners to resettle in the community. They had least success, on the other hand, in dealing with problematic drug use, helping ex-prisoners to obtain accommodation and providing them with emotional support. Objectives related to addressing or preventing offending behaviour were achieved totally or partially in just under two-thirds of cases. To the extent that direct comparisons can be made, these findings are broadly similar to those presented in the previous chapter.

Table 4.3: Objectives and social workers' views of the extent to which they were achieved

Objective	Number of cases	Percentage of cases	Number achieved	Percentage achieved[14]
Offending30	62%	19	63%	
Employment/education	21	44%	11	52%
Accommodation	18	38%	6	33%
Resettle in community	13	27%	9	69%
Alcohol	11	23%	8	73%
Family relationships	10	21%	6	60%
Personal relationships	8	17%	4	50%
Get through licence/conditions	8	17%	7	88%
Other practical issues[15]	8	17%	6	75%
Drug use 5	10%	1	20%	
Emotional support	5	10%	2	40%
Other factors related to offending[16]	5	10%	4	80%

EX-PRISONERS' RESPONSES TO THROUGHCARE

Social workers were asked to rate ex-prisoners according to how motivated they were to address their offending behaviour and to address other problems. As Table 4.4 reveals, just over a third of ex-prisoners were believed to have been highly motivated to address their offending and a further half were said to have been fairly motivated to do so. A quarter of the sample had been very motivated and two-thirds fairly motivated to address other problems. Less than a sixth of the sample had not been motivated to address their offending and only one in twelve had shown no motivation to address other problem areas in their lives.

Table 4.4: Social workers' views of ex-prisoners' motivation to address offending and other problems

How motivated	Address offending	Address other problems
Very	18	12
Fairly	23	32
Not at all	7	4
Total	48	48

There was a clear association between motivation to address offending and motivation to address other problems: ex-prisoners who were highly motivated to address their offending were most likely to be highly motivated to address other issues; whilst those who were least motivated to deal with their offending behaviour were also least motivated to address other problems. (Table 4.5)

Table 4.5: How motivated to address other problems by motivation to address offending

Address other problems	Address offending		
	Very	Fairly	Not at all
Very	11	0	1
Fairly	7	22	3
Not at all	0	1	3
Total	18	23	7

[14] Percentage of objectives achieved completely or to a significant extent.
[15] Financial issues (3) practical support (3) and use of leisure time (2).
[16] Violence (2) peer group (2) other attitudes supportive of offending (1).

Social workers were also asked to categorise their client's overall response to throughcare. Sixteen ex-prisoners (33 per cent) were thought to have shown a very positive response to throughcare and 19 (40 per cent) a fairly positive response. Ten (21 per cent) were said to have shown a mixed response and two (4 per cent) a fairly poor response. Only one ex-prisoner's response to throughcare was said to have been very poor.

Social workers were asked to identify factors which they believed had affected their client's response to throughcare. Factors identified as having adversely affected the client's response are summarised in Table 4.6. They fell in the main into four broad headings: the existence of other social or personal problems which detracted from the ex-prisoner's willingness or ability to comply (personal problems, drug use and social worker's inability to influence unemployment); reluctance on the part of the offender to engage with the social worker (did not want to be on licence, lack of interest, did not want to discuss past, unable to accept the impact of the offence on the victim); personal characteristics which undermined the possibility of a more positive response (lack of self esteem, immaturity); and the negative influence of offending peers.

Table 4.6: Social workers' views of the factors adversely affecting their client's response to throughcare

	Number of cases (n=13)
Personal problems	5
Did not want to be on licence	2
Peer relationships	2
Social worker's inability to influence employment	1
Lack of self-esteem	1
Lack of interest	1
Drug use	1
Immaturity	1
Did not want to discuss the past	1
Unable to accept the impact of offence on victim	1

Factors which were regarded as having consistently influenced ex-prisoners' responses in a positive way are summarised in Table 4.7. Most commonly clients were believed to have been motivated by their desire to avoid further offending or, more often, its likely consequences (including recall) or their wish to obtain help with various problems in their lives.

Stability within ex-prisoners' lives (as evidenced by the existence of supportive personal relationships and employment or, in one case, the absence more generally of problems) was also identified in a number of cases as having contributed to a positive response to community based throughcare. Features of the throughcare contact itself - the help received, the relationship established with the social worker or the clear framework provided by the licence - appeared in a smaller number of cases to have contributed to the ex-prisoner's positive response.

Table 4.7: Social workers' view of the factors positively influencing responses to throughcare

	Number of cases (n=35)
Motivated to address problems	13
Fear of consequences of further offending	7
Supportive relationships	6
Desire to avoid recall	5
Clear about expectations	4
Employment	4
Valued social work input	3
Motivated to stop offending	2
Relationship with social worker	2
Absence of personal problems	1

Turning now to what offenders were believed to have found most helpful about throughcare, the relevant responses are summarised in Table 4.8. Support of a practical or more general nature was most often referred to by social workers. Having someone to discuss their problems with and making progress in addressing their problems also featured significantly in the factors advanced by social workers in this respect.

Table 4.8: What social workers believed ex-prisoners found most helpful about throughcare

	Number of cases (n=41)
Practical support	12
Having someone to discuss problems with	11
Role of the social worker	8
General support	7
Making progress in addressing problems	4
Structure	3
Encouragement	2
Early release from custody	2
Reminder to avoid offending	1
Nothing	1

The role of the social worker was mentioned in a sixth of cases: this included the relationship established with the social worker (3 cases), knowledge that the social worker was available and responsive (3 cases) and the objectivity of the social worker (2 cases). Three offenders were believed to have valued the structure within which throughcare was provided: in two instances the regularity of contact with the social worker was believed to have been helpful while in a third the flexibility of appointments was mentioned as having been helpful for the ex-prisoner.

Those aspects of throughcare which offenders were believed to have found least helpful are summarised in Table 4.9. Reference was made most frequently to factors associated with the appointments themselves - their rigidity, frequency or location (usually office based). In five cases ex-prisoners were believed to have been disappointed by their social worker's inability to have a direct positive influence on practical issues such as accommodation or employment. The fact that social workers "had their hands tied" in relation to such practical issues was, as we shall see in the following chapter, a complaint often voiced by the ex-prisoners themselves.

Table 4.9: What social workers believed ex-prisoners found least helpful about throughcare

	Number of cases (n=27)
Nature of appointments	7
Social worker's inability to influence circumstances	5
Having attitudes or behaviour challenged	4
Intrusiveness	2
Specific areas of work	2
Being on licence in the first place	2
Reminder of the offence	2
The need to continue on order	1
Other residents	1
Nothing	3

Four ex-prisoners were believed to have resented having their behaviour or attitudes challenged by their social workers. Such resentment is, perhaps, not surprising when, as Chapter Five indicates, parolees in particular did not see the relevance of discussing their previous offending behaviour following their release. Another ex-prisoner was thought to have resented the constraints provided by statutory supervision on the basis that he "felt he'd served his time but was still not free" while the existence of a parole licence was said to have reinforced one ex-prisoner's view of himself as an offender.

THE IMPACT OF THROUGHCARE ON THE RISK OF RECIDIVISM

The final items in the social workers' questionnaire sought to elicit their views as to the risk of further offending presented by the ex-prisoner, whether that risk had changed since the offender had been released from custody and, if it had reduced, the extent to which social work intervention as opposed to other factors had contributed to the perceived reduction in risk. Certain findings presented in this section relate to a total of 46 cases: in two cases social workers were unable to offer an assessment of continued risk.

Risk of further offending

Thirty ex-prisoners (65 per cent) were thought unlikely to re-offend, 11 (24 per cent) were considered fairly likely re-offend and in five cases (11 per cent) further offending was believed by social workers to be very likely. The perceived risk of further offending was found to be related to ex-prisoners' willingness to address their offending and other problems and by their overall response to throughcare. More specifically, offenders who were described as having been highly motivated to address their offending and other problems and who were thought to have responded positively to throughcare were least likely to be considered at risk of committing offences in future.

Ex-prisoners under 26 years of age were more often thought to be at risk of further offending than were those aged 26 or over (45 per cent compared with 26 per cent). Whilst the numbers in each category were small, ex-prisoners in receipt of voluntary assistance were most often considered at risk of re-offending (six out of nine cases or 67 per cent) in comparison to statutory throughcare cases. Among the latter, parolees with additional requirements were more often thought at risk of further offending than other parolees and life licencees (six out of 15 or 40 per cent compared with two out of 12 or 17 per cent and one out of five or 20 per cent). These results, despite the small numbers, are nonetheless consistent with the observation in Chapter Two that voluntary cases tended to have more previous convictions and with the finding in Chapter Three that social workers more often focused upon offending behaviour in their supervision of parolees with additional requirements reflecting, it is suggested, their perception of a heightened risk of recidivism among this category of ex-prisoner.

In most instances social workers provided additional explanations for their assessment of risk in individual cases. In two cases, however, both of which involved sexual offenders, social workers were uncertain as to the risk the ex-prisoner continued to present:

> "[The ex-prisoner] understood the implications of his offending but has never denied his continued sexual attraction to children/young boys."

> "Very difficult to tell. Always a possibility."

In three of the five cases in which social workers believed the risk of further offending to be high, they pointed to continued offending as an indicator of continued risk. Homelessness, mental health problems and the ex-prisoner's immaturity were invoked to explain why, in two other cases, the ex-prisoner was very likely to re-offend.

> "He is very likely to re-offend as he lacks the maturity at present to deal with social/environmental factors and peer group influence. When he shows maturity, self reliance and independence he will then be able to choose whether to offend or not and when/if he reaches that point I believe he will stop offending."

In five of the 11 cases in which the ex-prisoner was considered fairly likely to re-offend reference was made to continued problematic alcohol or drug use. Relationship problems were referred to in three cases and lack of stability in the offender's circumstances in another three. Mention was made in individual cases of continued offending; continuing sexual fantasies, existence of a lifestyle supportive of offending; the possibility of the offender reacting under stress; and the offender's limited insight into his behaviour. In one case - involving a sexual offender - further offending was considered a possibility following termination of statutory supervision and the formal framework of controls it provided:

> "At the end of the licence [the ex-prisoner] had become involved in drugs again - purchased on the street. Domestic stability not attained."

> "As she has little or no insight into her offending and its impact on the victims it is possible that she will re-offend given the right circumstances."

> "[The ex-prisoner] continues to have problems with relationships and can 'bottle up' emotions so possibility of violent outbursts remains."

> "Client has had over ten years of an almost rootless existence. He is still struggling to settle down."

The majority of ex-prisoners were, however, considered unlikely to re-offend. The explanations offered by social workers in 29 of these 30 cases are summarised in Table 4.10 They fell broadly into four categories: the isolated nature of the original offence or the time which had elapsed since it occurred; offenders' motivation to avoid offending, including recognition of what they had to lose by continued offending, personal insight into their behaviour and the deterrent effect that imprisonment had had; the stability of the offender's current circumstances (in particular, personal or family relationships and employment); and improvements in the offender's circumstances since the commission of the original offence. For example:

"Client spent lengthy time in prison and spoke of determination to avoid it given experience. Also little apparent problems in life likely to place at risk of involvement in offending."

"[The ex-prisoner] has found prison to have been traumatic and has shown a marked degree of maturity since being involved in throughcare."

"Client did not have a history of involvement in offending behaviour or violent behaviour for which he was given custody. He found it difficult to come to terms with his offence."

"[The ex-prisoner] does not appear to have had a history of persistent offending prior to custody and seems motivated to get on with his life re employment and personal relationships."

"Now in full time employment in a job he enjoys. In addition he seems to have addressed his drug problems and has a very supportive family."

"I would think [the ex-prisoner] has too much going for him now to contemplate risking it for the sake of re-offending."

"Client committed offence of murder 13 years ago - not necessarily part of a more general criminal culture. Has managed not to offend over last two years. Also appears to know what he has to do to remain free of offending."

"He has been accepted by his partner's very supportive family with no history of offending. Now has something to 'live up to'."

Table 4.10: Reasons for being considered unlikely to re-offend

	Number of cases (n=29)
No real history of offending	8
Personal/family relationships/responsibilities	7
Prison sentence served as a deterrent	6
Employment	6
Control over alcohol use	4
Maturity	4
Motivated to avoid offending	4
Crime committed some time ago	4
Circumstances surrounding offence unlikely to recur	3
Aware of what she/he has to lose	3
Control over drug use	2
Has insight into behaviour	2
Circumstances have improved	2
Avoids offending peers	2
Few personal problems	1
Has developed new interests	1

Changes in risk of re-offending

In addition to assessing the current risk of re-offending, social workers were asked to indicate whether that risk had changed since the offender had been provided with community based throughcare. In 23 cases (48 per cent) the risk of recidivism was believed to be unchanged. Thirteen ex-prisoners (27 per cent) were thought to be slightly less at risk of re-offending and eight (17 per cent) to be at much less risk. Only four ex-prisoners

(8 per cent) were considered to present a greater risk of re-offending, three of whom were believed to be slightly more at risk of recidivism and one much more so. Each of these four ex-prisoners had been subject to a parole licence with additional requirements, which tends to add some support to the argument previously presented that this category of ex-prisoner was somewhat riskier, on the whole, than the other groups. This perception of risk was no doubt a critical factor in the Parole Board's decision to attach additional requirements to the parole licence.

Just under half the sample were considered to be less at risk of re-offending than they were on release from custody while in a similar proportion of cases the risk of recidivism was thought to be unchanged. One in 12 ex-prisoners were thought to be more likely to re-offend since their release. In the case of the offender who was believed to be much more likely to re-offend, the social worker explained that:

> "[The ex-prisoner's] domestic status deteriorated. Couldn't cope with mother's address or relationship with girlfriend. Concerns in respect of mental health but [the ex-prisoner] is not keeping appointments with GP."

In two of the three cases in which re-offending was believed to be slightly more likely compared with when the offender was released, the removal of the formal controls provided by statutory supervision was said to be a significant factor. In the third case the social worker explained that the "main risk is [the ex-prisoner's] involvement in 'street drugs' again".

Only six of the offenders whose risk of recidivism was unchanged were believed to present a risk of re-offending. In two cases the ex-prisoner had continued to offend since being released from custody. Other explanations offered in individual cases included the fact that the offending behaviour was deeply entrenched; the offender's immaturity; homelessness; the ex-prisoner's refusal to engage with the social worker and the fact that specialist treatment resources had not been obtained.

The other offenders in this category were thought not to be at risk of further offending. In other words, they were not considered to present a risk of recidivism on release and were no more likely now to re-offend. Explanations, as Table 4.11 illustrates, tended to focus upon the fact that the offender's lifestyle was settled, motivation to avoid further offending and the one-off nature of the original offence.

Table 4.11: Reasons why further offending was still unlikely

	Number of cases (n=17)
Motivated to avoid offending	5
Settled lifestyle/circumstances	3
Employment	3
Circumstances surrounding the offence unlikely to recur	3
Maturity	2
Family support/responsibilities	2
Deterrent effect of prison	1
Time elapsed since the commission of the offence	1
Responded well to supervision	1
First offender	1

In some instances social workers stressed that factors other than throughcare had had a positive impact upon the ex-prisoner's motivation to avoid further offending. One social worker, for example, explained that "supervision had little impact on ex-prisoner's own views and determination" while another suggested that "the reasons for non-offending are probably more likely to have had a deterrent effect than the throughcare had".

It is interesting to compare these findings with those obtained in the study of probation supervision which was undertaken as part of the same research programme. In that study, the fact that a probationer's risk of re-offending remained unchanged was considered to indicate a negative outcome of supervision. This illustrates quite sharply a key difference between throughcare and probation supervision and one which was substantiated by the offenders themselves in both studies: whereas probation is viewed as being essentially concerned with reducing the risk of further offending, a focus upon offending behaviour with a view to risk reduction is less likely to be viewed, particularly by those subject to it, as being appropriate in the context of throughcare supervision. Instead, supervision is regarded as an opportunity for the ex-prisoner to be offered practical assistance as a means of resettling in the community.

There was, however, a significant proportion of ex-prisoners who were believed, following a period of community based throughcare, to present less risk of re-offending than when they were initially released. The explanations offered by social workers in these cases are summarised in Table 4.12. In almost two-thirds of cases further offending was believed to be less likely than when the individuals were first released from prison because they had gained further insight into their offending behaviour and its consequences. Indeed, such increased self awareness - or, as one social worker described it, "willingness to look at behaviour and actions with a view to further prevention" - appears to be the key factor in distinguishing those whose risk of offending remained low throughout and those whose risk had decreased since their return to the community.

"He is more aware now of the effect his behaviour has on his family and on his life."

"I believe he is less likely to re-offend because he has been encouraged to examine his actions and by doing so is more self-aware. This is a first step towards ending offending rather than the complete answer."

"[The ex-prisoner] is very clear what the implications of his offending are and to some extent the cognitive distortions necessary to offend."

"He has learned that he must exercise personal responsibility and consider the effect his behaviour has on his family circle."

Table 4.12: Reasons for a reduced risk of re-offending

	Number of cases (n=18)
Increased understanding of offending and its consequences	11
Motivated to avoid offending/imprisonment	5
Settled circumstances	4
Control of alcohol/drug use	3

The contribution of throughcare to the reduction of risk

Twenty-one ex-prisoners in total were believed to be less at risk of re-offending since being released from custody. To what extent was throughcare, as opposed to other factors, believed to have contributed to the perceived reduction in risk? In the vast majority of cases where the risk of offending was perceived to have reduced (19 out of 21), throughcare was considered to have played some part in achieving that reduction in risk: in four of these cases it was believed to have played a significant part and in 15 cases some part. In only two cases was the perceived reduction in risk of recidivism believed to have been totally unrelated to the provision of community based throughcare services. Overall, therefore, throughcare was thought to have contributed to a reduced risk of re-offending in approximately two-fifths of cases (19 out of 48) in the sample.

SOCIAL WORKERS' COMMENTS ON THROUGHCARE

Social workers were given an opportunity to offer additional comments on individual cases. In six cases social workers stressed that the effectiveness of throughcare was ultimately dependent upon the motivation of the ex-prisoner:

"I would assess it as being ineffective in this case due to client's lack of motivation. Initially motivation was high while client gained help with benefits etc. Since this was a voluntary contract there was little to be gained beyond this."

"As in a lot of cases I think effectiveness may be linked to motivation. This client was obviously motivated to lead an offending free lifestyle."

In five cases social workers emphasised the positive function of throughcare while in three others throughcare was believed to have had little positive impact upon the offender:

"Throughcare gave client opportunity to address the problem areas in his life. Also the fact that throughcare is based in local community was also advantageous."

"Throughcare helps the client to focus more on his behaviour and change aspects which could lead to a recall to prison."

"We have recommended probation in past and it was discounted by court at the time. Client not that much further on."

Four social workers emphasised the importance of material improvements in their clients' circumstances as having had a positive influence on their ability to avoid re-offending and resettle in the community:

> "Getting a house and a job gives him a better chance than hours talking about himself with a social worker."

> "[The ex-prisoner] returned to community to own tenancy and good family support which made things easier for him."

One social worker described throughcare as "statutory provision of someone to talk to", another emphasised the controlling element of throughcare in the case of a Schedule 1 offender ("he knew he was being monitored and this did affect his behaviour") and two others explained that they had undertaken little more than a monitoring function in the particular case:

> "Parole supervision - little effect. Client had few apparent issues to deal with and supervision was undertaken on an 'ensuring compliance and appointment keeping' basis only towards the end."

> "More a holding case - prison provided reasons not to offend before throughcare."

Three social workers, finally, suggested that the lack of necessary resources had limited the effectiveness of throughcare supervision:

> "Community based throughcare can be an effective way of working. However quite often it is difficult to provide this service from a resource point of view. i.e. there are other competing statutory demands."

> "It is possible that if we had had more time to work with him in custody we could have prepared him better for his release into the community."

SUMMARY

Social workers and their clients were believed by the former to be generally agreed as to the main issues in a case, though social workers were more likely to consider problematic drug or alcohol use as issues requiring attention while their clients were thought more likely to attach significance to financial problems and to employment/education. Whilst offending behaviour was the issue most often identified as being significant by social workers, ex-prisoners were thought most likely to attach importance to accommodation and employment.

Avoiding or addressing offending featured as an objective in just over three-fifths of cases. This was followed by employment/education, accommodation, helping the offender to resettle in the community, alcohol and family relationships. Social workers appeared to make greatest progress in relation to alcohol use, the provision of general practical support and helping ex-prisoners to resettle in the community. They had least success in dealing with problematic drug use, helping ex-prisoners to obtain accommodation and providing them with emotional support.

The majority of ex-prisoners were said by social workers to have been motivated to address their offending and other problems. Three-quarters of the sample were believed to have responded positively to throughcare. Factors which were believed by social workers to have adversely affected ex-prisoners' responses to throughcare included the existence of social or personal problems which detracted from the ex-prisoner's ability or willingness to comply; reluctance on the part of the offender to engage with the social worker; the personal characteristics of the offender; and the influence of offending peers. Ex-prisoners' responses to throughcare were believed by their social workers to have been influenced positively by their motivation to avoid further offending and its consequences; by stability in ex-prisoners' lives; and by features of the throughcare contact itself - the help received, the relationship established with the social worker or the clear framework provided by a statutory licence.

Ex-prisoners were believed to have most valued practical or general support and the opportunity to discuss their problems. The role of the social worker was also mentioned in a sixth of cases. Features of the appointments themselves were most often thought to have been found by ex-prisoners as unhelpful. Five offenders were believed to have been disappointed by their social worker's inability to have a direct positive influence on matters such as employment or accommodation.

Two thirds of ex-prisoners were believed unlikely to re-offend, a quarter were thought fairly likely to re-offend and in one in nine cases further offending was considered very likely. Offenders who were described as highly motivated to address their offending and other problems were least likely to be considered at some risk of committing offences in future. Younger offenders were thought more often to present a risk of continued offending than those aged 26 years or older. Offenders subject to voluntary supervision were more often than those subject to statutory community based throughcare to present a risk of further offending. Amongst the latter, parolees who had additional requirements attached to their licencees were perceived to present the greatest risk. Risk of continued offending was indicated by continued offending during the period on throughcare, by the existence of problematic alcohol or drug use or other factors associated with offending or by general instability in the ex-prisoners' lives.

In providing reasons why ex-prisoners were unlikely to re-offend social workers made reference to the isolated nature of the original offence or the time that had elapsed since its commission; offenders' motivation to avoid offending and its consequences; the stability of the ex-prisoner's circumstances; and improvements in the offender's circumstances since the commission of the original offence.

Forty-four per cent of the sample were considered by their social workers to be less at risk of re-offending compared with when they were released from custody, while in 48 per cent of cases the risk of recidivism was thought not to have changed. In four cases - each of which pertained to ex-prisoners subject to parole licences with additional requirements - the risk of re-offending was believed to have increased: in two of these cases social workers suggested that the removal of formal controls provided by statutory supervision was a significant factor.

Most offenders whose risk of recidivism was thought not to have changed were not considered to be at risk of further offending. In other words, they were not considered to have presented a risk of recidivism on release and were thought no more likely now to re-offend. Reference was made to prisoners' settled lifestyles, their motivation to avoid further offending and the one-off nature of the original offence.

In two-thirds of cases in which further offending was believed to be less likely and social workers offered a explanation for their assessment, it was suggested ex-prisoners had gained further insight into their offending behaviour and its consequences since being released from prison. Indeed, such increased self-awareness appeared to be the key factor which distinguished those whose risk of re-offending remained low throughout and those whose risk had decreased since returning to the community.

Twenty-one ex-prisoners were considered to be at less risk of re-offending since being released from custody. Throughcare was believed by social workers to have contributed to some extent in achieving a reduction in risk in 15 cases and was thought to have played a significant part in four others. Overall, therefore, throughcare was thought to have contributed to a reduced risk of re-offending in approximately 40 per cent (19 out of 48) of cases in the sample.

CHAPTER FIVE

EX-PRISONERS' EXPERIENCES AND VIEWS OF COMMUNITY BASED THROUGHCARE

INTRODUCTION

Interviews were conducted with 31 ex-prisoners who had been in receipt of social work supervision or support on release from custody: four in Burns, 15 in Bruce, nine in Scott and three in Wallace. The interview sample consisted of 24 adult ex-prisoners and seven ex-prisoners under 21 years of age. Sixteen ex-prisoners had been subject to parole (in five cases with additional requirement), five were life licencees, four had been subject to statutory after-care and six had been in receipt of voluntary assistance from the social work department.

THE PERCEIVED PURPOSE OF THROUGHCARE

Looking back to when they were first released on licence, most ex-prisoners who were subject to statutory supervision saw the social work supervision as an integral part of the prison sentence, but this did not lessen their expectations in relation to the social work support they might receive. Quite the contrary: the majority had very high (albeit, many thought, unrealistic) expectations of the "support" element of the licence. When asked what they understood would be expected of them on licence, around half the respondents recognised the need to avoid further offending and one-third mentioned that they had to keep appointments with their supervising social worker. Nine ex-prisoners expected social work support if needed and seven saw parole as merely a monitoring or surveillance exercise.

The main commitment that respondents believed social workers expected of them was to keep appointments (14). Whilst 15 felt that keeping out of trouble was a key issue, only four thought that social workers actually stipulated this at the outset. However, eight ex-prisoners felt that support was specifically offered by social workers during the initial discussions about throughcare. When respondents were asked to explain the purpose of parole and what it was meant to achieve, 18 saw it as a "carrot and stick" - a reward for good behaviour within custody and a chance to prove one's worth on release. Seventeen people further saw it as a deterrent to re-offending and 12 viewed parole as a stepping stone towards re-integration into the community. In this respect, several described their community based social worker as a key link in the transition between the prison and the community.

Fourteen ex-prisoners believed that one of the primary purposes of community based throughcare should be to provide social work support of a proactive nature and, by inference, more to meet practical than emotional needs. Those in receipt of voluntary assistance on release expected nothing but social work support, given the non-supervisory nature of their involvement with the social work department. Expectations of what social work supervision might or should involve did not differ between life licencees and those subject to shorter periods of statutory aftercare or parole.

The study did not set out to enquire why people applied for early release, but from general discussions with respondents, it would appear that most of the sample who had been granted it believed that parole per se was an effective or attractive option because it was a reward for good behaviour in prison and a deterrent to further offending once released. Although this would still appear to have been the majority view with hindsight, one ex-prisoner remarked that:

> "If [parole] had been any longer I think I'd have handed myself back in, to be honest with you. It was easier in jail sometimes, you wouldn't have to worry about where your next meal was coming from". (38 year old male)

SOCIAL WORK INVOLVEMENT PRIOR TO RELEASE

Prison Social Workers

Overall, ex-prisoners' experiences of prison social work were generally viewed as unhelpful. There was a belief, expressed by 14 ex-prisoners, that prison social workers were untrustworthy or uninterested. When asked

"What did your social worker do to help you [before release]?", 14 respondents cited help that they had received from prison social workers, compared to 22 who cited instances of help received from the community based social worker prior to release.

Twelve respondents cited instances of constructive help by prison social workers in matters relating to the terms of parole, housing, money, offending and future job prospects. This help was, it appeared, gratefully received. Nevertheless, only eight respondents could think of additional help they would have welcomed from prison social workers compared with 22 who could not. Additional help which would have been appreciated included advice on housing and future prospects. One ex-prisoner would have appreciated the prison social workers being more interested and another suggested that they should be less judgmental. Five respondents would have appreciated help from the prison social worker but did not request it. This was mainly because they felt that prison social workers were not the appropriate (or most convenient) source of such support:

> "The prison social workers, you feel as if they just want to know things and it will get relayed back to the screws. I know all social workers are meant to be the same but a lot of the boys get the feeling that the screws know a lot more than they're meant to know, so you don't really trust [the prison social workers]". (27 year old male)

> "[Prison social workers] were working for the system, not for the person". (23 year old male)

As well as feeling that prison social workers were unhelpful or untrustworthy, some respondents specifically stated that prison social workers were more interested in lifers and sex offenders than other prisoners (2); that you had to accept guilt for your crime before a prison social worker would engage with you (1); that the procedure for requesting to see them was time-consuming and obstructive (1); that they were not "street-wise" (2) and that they did not/could not treat your requests necessarily in confidence (3). Whilst it is difficult to pinpoint precise criticisms, there was a majority view that community based social workers were more appropriate and more amenable than prison social workers in dealing with issues raised by prisoners.

Others suggested that the insular or detached nature of prison life itself made prison social workers less effective than community based social workers in liaising with the outside world. Prison social workers, it was suggested, were not well placed to become familiarised or liaise with agencies on the outside. Others thought that such liaison was not within the prison social workers' remit or that their hands were otherwise tied in terms of being able to offer practical support in preparation for release.

Community based Social Workers

Respondents were asked about the frequency and utility of visits by community based social workers prior to release. Whilst several prisoners were able or required to see their social worker during periods of home leave, 21 received one or more visits from a community based social worker within the prison. Twelve had such visits once or twice, four a few times and five on a regular basis. Four of the five who had visits on a regular basis were seen by staff from a dedicated throughcare project who visited local prisons regularly and took the opportunity to see several prisoners on the same visit, offering practical support and support for the prisoner's family.

The often distant location of the prison from the prisoner's address on release was viewed by some prisoners as having limited the opportunities for contact with their community based social worker while still in prison. For many respondents the parole process itself often precluded such visits because of the limited time available between parole being granted and the actual liberation date. Some prisoners were told only days before release that their application of some months back had been successful, and in one instance the prisoner was informed of his parole date the evening before he was released. Such timing obviously restricts the capacity of both prison based and community based social workers to work proactively on the ex-prisoner's behalf to ease the transition back into the community.

During prison visits, the two main topics discussed with community based social workers were general release plans (cited by 13 respondents) and housing (10). Other matters discussed included job prospects, family or personal relationships, personal problems and other practical problems relating to release. In Bruce, where the availability of supported accommodation attracted more of the otherwise rootless ex-prisoners, accommodation and general plans for re-integration were a priority area of discussion. Whilst views were mixed as to how helpful these visits were, more than half the ex-prisoners' interviewed (17) could think of no other ways that the community based social worker could have helped at that point in time. Of the nine respondents who would have valued additional support prior to release, five felt that housing advice was the key issue.

Three-way meetings - involving the prisoner, the prison social worker and the community based social worker - seemed to occur prior to release in 12 cases. Nineteen ex-prisoners, on the other hand, could not recollect such a meeting taking place. In only one case was mention made by the ex-prisoner of a written agreement about areas of work to be addressed on parole having been drawn up prior to release. The limited time available between parole being granted and the actual release date was often, it appears, not conducive to forward planning of this nature. Even life licencees considered that more pre-release planning could have been undertaken, with two suggesting that the English procedure for parole was more systematic and thorough in terms of supervising officers helping to prepare prisoners for release.

Nine of the ten prisoners who did not receive a personal visit from a community-based social worker while in custody thought that visits should have taken place on a regular basis to keep the prisoner in touch with life on the outside, to get to know the ex-prisoner and to offer advice on housing or other practical issues.

SOCIAL WORK SUPERVISION AND SUPPORT FOLLOWING RELEASE

Ex-prisoners generally believed that they were in accordance with their social workers that drugs or alcohol, employment, re-integration, family or personal relationships and financial matters were among the most pressing issues to be addressed following release.

The most immediate issue for ex-prisoners themselves was housing. Accommodation was identified as a problem by 14 ex-prisoners but only eight believed that it was recognised by social workers as an issue requiring attention. Conversely, 12 respondents said that re-offending was an issue that social workers wanted to address but only five respondents believed at that stage that it was an issue themselves.

Respondents' recall of their first visit to the social worker on release was that it was generally "about right" in terms of timing. Twelve thought they were seen on the day of release, seven were seen the next day and 11 were seen within a week. The minority who thought their appointment was too soon believed that they needed more time to see their families and to attend to immediate practical matters, particularly those relating to money.

Only three ex-prisoners could not think of any problems facing them on release. The remainder commonly cited housing (14), money (12) and general problems of re-integration (9). Other problems included offending, peer group influence, family or personal relationships, unemployment and drugs or alcohol. Two further problems which were thought to have impeded re-integration were "paranoia"[17] (cited by 7 respondents) and unwarranted attention by the police (cited by 5 respondents). As one ex-prisoner explained:

> "A lot of boys when they come out, they feel threatened by the police's presence... They know you're an offender and they just want to push you to the limit. If they backed off a lot, there wouldn't be so many ex-cons re-offending". (27 year old male)

The feelings of paranoia were especially acute amongst the life licencees. One described his initial bemusement that people in a busy city street were not all walking in the same direction and the difficulty he experienced in restraining himself from responding aggressively towards anyone who inadvertently bumped into him. The sense of paranoia was also exacerbated, for those who were homeless, by the tensions arising from having to share hostel accommodation with strangers who themselves had a variety of problems. Lifers in particular were acutely aware of the need to exercise patience and tact and to avoid potentially escalatory or confrontational situations. As one 34 year old explained, "It's like walking on ice all the time".

Length and frequency of contact

Just under half the ex-prisoners (13) who were asked their opinion on the length of their involvement with social workers following release from custody thought it had been too long. Ten believed the length of time had been about right and six felt it was too short. The latter were mostly on short-term parole licences of four to six months duration. All five lifers believed that life licences should, instead, be of two to five years duration in total.

In terms of the frequency of appointments, 14 ex-prisoners believed that the level of contact was about right, while eight thought that they had been required to see their social worker too often and six thought they had not seen their social worker often enough. Some of the latter group would, it appeared, have welcomed a more systematic arrangement, with appointments being initiated by the social worker rather than being initiated by the ex-prisoner as and when problems arose.

---

[17] Paranoia was, in the main, the word used by respondents to describe the feeling many ex-prisoners have of being stared at or in some way discriminated against within the community. It also incorporated the fear and vulnerability felt over the possibility and indeterminate nature of recall.

Help provided in the context of throughcare

In the course of interview respondents were asked to indicate what they had hoped to achieve from throughcare and to rate, on a five point scale, the extent to which each of their objectives had been achieved. The resultant responses are summarised in Table 5.1.

Table 5.1: Ex-prisoners' objectives and the extent to which they were achieved

Objectives	Totally/to a significant extent	Partially	To a limited extent/not at all	Total
Employment/education	6	7	9	22
Accommodation	5	4	5	14
Resettle in community	8	2	1	11
Offending	6	0	3	9
Other practical issues	4	1	4	9
Relationships	6	2	0	8
Drug/alcohol use	5	1	2	8
Personal development	4	1	1	6
Financial	1	1	3	5

Resettling in the community, avoiding further offending and family or personal relationships were the objectives most likely to have been achieved totally or to a significant extent. Financial objectives, those relating to employment or education and those relating to accommodation were, on the other hand, most likely to have been achieved only partially, to a limited extent or not at all.

In terms of the help provided by social workers, 22 ex-prisoners said their social worker referred them to, or liaised on their behalf with, other agencies. In 17 cases the referral or liaison was related to accommodation. Twenty indicated that they talked to or got advice from their social worker, and eight received help or advice in relation to welfare benefits. Whilst 14 ex-prisoners were unable to identify any further help that their social workers might have given them ("their hands are tied"), ten would have appreciated more help in contacting other agencies (in seven cases housing-related) and five in finding a job while five would have welcomed more regular contact and general support from their social worker. Nine ex-prisoners considered that their situation had improved as a direct result of social work advice or intervention, but 22 felt that things had not improved or they themselves had achieved the change on their own.

Several ex-prisoners seemed unsure about the presence or otherwise of additional requirements to their licence. Where these were known to exist, they related mainly to drug or alcohol counselling, which respondents tended to find helpful and flexible.

The social worker's approach

As with probationers in another study in the same research programme, the features of their social worker's approach which ex-prisoners found most helpful were that they were easy to talk to (17), easygoing (11) and straightforward (9). The fact that they cared (7 felt that they did and 7 that they did not) and could be relied upon was considered important:

> "I knew that... if I had a big, massive, raging argument with anybody in my house and stormed out, I always knew that I could sort of rely on [the social worker] to help me in some sort of way". (21 year old male)

Having the time - "being there for me" as one 27 year old put it - was equally important. Seven ex-prisoners had gained the impression that the social worker was too busy to give them much time:

> "I know they're busy people, but they should be there for you when you need to see them". (22 year old male)

As with probationers, ex-prisoners generally found approaches which were intended to "empower" the ex-prisoner somewhat unhelpful. Instead, these respondents would have preferred the social worker to be more proactive and directive, especially with those who felt the need for that kind of guidance:

> "You want someone to sit down and sort it out with you". (38 year old male)

"[Parole] was there to try and get you back into the community but they just tell you 'go and do this', but how are you meant to just go and do it when you haven't got a clue. Seventeen months I was lying in Polmont, and they tell you to go and get a job. I didn't even know where to start". (19 year old male)

Ex-prisoners appeared to appreciate social workers who showed interest in them and appeared to care, who did not attempt to pressurise them and who were there when needed. By contrast, seven probationers suggested that their social workers did not convey the impression of caring, four expressed disappointment that social workers had limited powers to influence their circumstances, three had reservations about how confidential the service offered by the social work department was and three complained that their social workers had not given them the practical help they required.

The majority of ex-prisoners (21) believed that, overall, their social worker had been helpful though ten thought they had not. Those who thought that their social worker had been helpful made reference to the fact that the social worker was there when needed, was someone to talk to and was a useful link between the prison and the community. Nine, on the other hand, believed that their involvement with social workers was too intrusive or time-consuming.

When asked if they had changed in any way as a result of their community based throughcare contact, 18 ex-prisoners reported that it had made no difference, seven thought that their contact with their social worker had helped to some extent and four indicated that it had made them more disillusioned about the efficacy of social work support. Fifteen ex-prisoners believed that they had gained nothing from their experience of throughcare, with only 11 stating that they had gained something from social work support. Though 17 ex-prisoners were unable to identify other types of support or assistance that their social worker might usefully have provided, 13 others said that they would have welcomed more practical advice and support.

The ideal social worker

The significance of practical support was highlighted when ex-prisoners were invited to take on the hypothetical role of social worker and to outline the key issues that they consider it important to address. All made reference to the need for the social worker to address practical problems facing the ex-prisoner, with particular emphasis being placed on accommodation, employment, drug or alcohol misuse and financial matters. Respondents also attached importance to the need for the social worker to spend time with and get to know the ex-prisoner and his/her family (through, for example, more prison visits prior to release and more home visits thereafter). Listening and talking to the ex-prisoner were likewise considered important as was providing help with issues defined as relevant by the ex-prisoners themselves. Respondents stressed the need for the ex-prisoner to want help in the first place for social work intervention to be effective and to effect any meaningful change. Some suggested that social workers could not, unless they had first-hand experience of problems, understand what the ex-prisoner was going through:

"I don't like social workers because they just don't understand people's problems. I mean they say 'I understand what you're going through', but how could she understand what I went through, she's been sitting on her arse in an office for the past 12 years". (38 year old male, lifer).

Focusing upon offending behaviour was viewed as important by eight ex-prisoners in the hypothetical role of social worker. Invariably, however, respondents considered the main priority to be helping the prisoner settle back into the community through the provision of practical support.

OFFENDING BEHAVIOUR

"So what's the point of me going to see a social worker if I've not got a fucking problem. If I'm going to re-offend, I'm going to re-offend. It doesn't matter if there's a social worker there or not. He tells me to come out and see him every week, I say 'What for? What for?'. It gets you up tight, it's soaking wet, I get out my bed, 'I'm doing all right, I'll see you later'. There's no need for that. If you've got a problem.... I think you should go and see him and make your own appointment. If I re-offend and go to jail, he'll be notified right away". (35 year old male)

The National Standards suggest that in helping ex-prisoners to resettle into the community, social workers should assist them:

...to understand, recognise and tackle positively those aspects of attitude, behaviour and pressures which contributed to past offending and the most recent custodial sentence. (SWSG, 1991, para. 72.1)

While seven ex-prisoners thought that offending might still be a problem which they wanted to address on release, others felt that offending was an irrelevant issue raised frequently by the social worker. Eight considered their offence to have been an isolated incident and suggested that to focus on offending following release was an unnecessary distraction when what they needed was practical support. Equally, for those for whom re-offending was a possibility, there was a majority view that it was up to the individual to stop and that social work intervention could, at best, have only a marginal impact in this respect:

> "It doesn't matter what a social worker says or tries to do for that person. If they still want to take drugs and have a life of crime, they will". (22 year old male)

Focusing on offending through the medium of exercises/questionnaires was cited as having occurred in five cases, but the majority of ex-prisoners merely talked with their social worker about their offending and nine could not recall having discussed it at all.

Each of the 31 respondents offered a view as to their continued risk of re-offending. The majority (25) believed it was unlikely that they would re-offend, while one in eight (4) thought that further offending was fairly likely and two ex-prisoners thought it was very likely. Social workers had completed questionnaires in 28 of these cases, permitting a comparison of social workers' and ex-prisoners' perceptions of risk. Of the 16 cases in which social workers believed further offending to be unlikely, 15 ex-prisoners shared this assessment: the remaining prisoner thought it fairly likely that he would re-offend. Two of the nine prisoners whom social workers believed were fairly likely to re-offend shared this assessment: five believed that they were unlikely to re-offend while two thought that further offending was very likely. On the other hand, none of the three prisoners whom social workers perceived as having a high risk of further offending considered this to be the case: one believed that he was fairly likely to re-offend and two that re-offending was unlikely. Social workers and ex-prisoners were, therefore, agreed in their assessment of risk in 17 out of 28 cases. In three of the remaining 11 cases social workers tended to perceive a lower level of risk than did ex-prisoners while in eight cases the reverse was true.

Compared with when they were first released from prison, four-fifths of the sample (25) considered themselves now to be much less likely to re-offend while three thought that the risk of offending was unchanged and two believed themselves to be at a greater risk of re-offending than when they were first released. No information was available in respect of one respondent who has been excluded from the following analysis.

The 25 ex-prisoners who considered themselves now to be at less risk of re-offending were asked to indicate the extent to which throughcare, as opposed to other factors, had contributed to this reduction in risk. While nine ex-prisoners believed that their social work contact had had some impact upon their risk of further offending, only four considered it to have made a significant contribution. Overall it would appear that throughcare was perceived to have had no impact on the likelihood of re-offending by three-fifths (18 out of 30) of respondents.

One respondent was unable to identify factors other than being on throughcare which had made it less likely that he would re-offend. Twenty-four others, however, offered a variety of explanations as to why their risk of further offending had decreased. These are summarised in Table 5.2.

Table 5.2: Why respondents were less likely to re-offend

	Number of cases (n=24)
Motivated to stop offending	11
Personal relationships/responsibilities	10
Employment/education	8
Wish to avoid letting family down	7
Friends	5
Getting older	4
Control over drug use	3
Settled lifestyle	3

Almost half of this group of ex-prisoners emphasised the importance of their own determination to avoid further offending. The importance of personal relationships with partners or family and a desire to avoid the consequences of continued offending for their families also featured prominently. Several ex-prisoners pointed to increased stability in their lives (through, for example, having obtained employment or access to education or having gained control over former misuse of drugs). Five respondents suggested that the influence of friends was important: three because they had made a conscious effort to distance themselves from offending peers and two because they did not want to let their (non-offending) friends down. Finally, four ex-prisoners pointed to their increased maturity - the fact that they were "getting older" - as a reason for being less likely in future to re-offend.

OVERALL IMPRESSIONS OF THROUGHCARE

Eight respondents left prison to take up supported accommodation - often much needed and appreciated by life licencees and sex offenders who might otherwise be rootless immediately on release. However, several problems faced those moving from long-term prison sentences into supported accommodation. There was often confusion, in the ex-prisoner's eyes, between the role of the keyworker and that of the supervising officer. The keyworker, who had day-to-day contact with the ex-prisoner, tended to assume responsibility for those practical tasks associated with the re-integration of the ex-prisoner into the community while the social worker supervising the licence assumed more of a monitoring role.

Whereas 11 ex-prisoners were generally positive about their throughcare experience, the majority (20) gave a negative rating of the experience, either because they felt they did not get any practical help or because they were not convinced of the sincerity or the ability of the social worker responsible for the provision of supervision and support. This said, many tended to blame social workers for problems - related, for example, to unemployment or housing - which were more structural in nature and in respect of which social workers had limited powers to intervene. The difficulties faced by many ex-prisoners on release were summed up by one respondent as follows:

> "...for a start, a con coming out should have a house, he shouldn't have money problems. If they're giving him parole, see the moment you come out the jail, your cheque should be there, then you can go and see your social worker right away without any hassle. But DHSS, everybody coming out of prison seems to get knocked back for their money. And then they've got to appeal. And that could take three to four weeks before you get your money and that's no use to you if you've got nobody.... Alright maybe you don't deserve it, but if the system's there for them to help you, they should be doing it. It's like every department is fighting against each other. The Housing have got their policies, the DHSS have got their policies, the Social Work Department can only do so much, their hands are tied.... If they're going to be helpful at all to prisoners coming out to stop them re-offending, there should be one system - 'there's a grant, there's accommodation and there's a job club that you attend to look for work'. There should only be one department". (35 year old male)

SUMMARY

Most of those subject to release on licence had high expectations of the social work support they might receive though seven saw parole as merely a monitoring or surveillance exercise. Eighteen parolees viewed parole as a reward for good behaviour while in custody and a chance to prove one's worth on release. Seventeen further saw it as a deterrent to re-offending and 12 regarded parole as a stepping stone towards re-integration into the community.

Although some respondents were able to cite examples of constructive help they had received from prison based social workers, prison social work input was more generally viewed as unhelpful either because social workers were seen as untrustworthy or uninterested or because the insular or detached nature of prison life made prison social workers less effective in liaising with the outside world.

Just over two-thirds of the sample had received one or more visits from their community based social worker in prison; just over a third were able to recall having had a three-way meeting with the prison based and community based social worker. In some instances the distance of the prison from home or the limited time available between parole being granted and the date of release had precluded such visits. The main topics discussed at pre-release meetings were general release plans and accommodation. Other issues included employment, family relationships, personal problems and other practical problems relating to release. Views were mixed as to the helpfulness of these visits. Those who would have wanted more support at this stage generally believed that housing was the key issue. Most ex-prisoners who had had no contact with their community based social worker prior to release would have valued such contact.

Respondents were generally of the view that there was agreement between themselves and their social workers as to what constituted the most pressing issues to address following release. The areas in which the greatest divergence of views was thought to exist were accommodation and offending behaviour: social workers, it was suggested, tended to underestimate the significance of the former and overplay the importance of the latter.

Most ex-prisoners believed that the timing of their first post-release interview was about right. A few who thought that their first appointment was too soon would have welcomed more time to see their families and sort out immediate practical matters such as money. The types of help offered by social workers included liaison with other agencies and the provision of support and advice. Just under half the sample could not think of any other help that social workers could have given them. However ten would have appreciated more help in contacting other agencies (usually housing-related), five would have welcomed assistance in finding a job and five would have valued more regular contact and support.

Overall, nine ex-prisoners believed that their situation had improved as a direct result of social work advice or intervention but 22 thought that their circumstances had not improved or, if they had, that they themselves had achieved the change on their own. When asked what they had hoped to achieve from community based throughcare, respondents most often cited employment or education, accommodation and resettling in the community. Fewer than a third mentioned the avoidance of further offending as an explicit objective. Resettling in the community, avoiding further offending and help with family or personal relationships were the objectives thought most likely to have been achieved completely or to a significant extent. Financial objectives, those related to employment or education and those relating to accommodation were, on the other hand, most likely to have been achieved only partially, to a limited extent or not at all.

Just under half the sample believed that their contact with social workers was too long whilst a fifth (mostly on very short parole licences) believed it to have been too short. All five life licencees believed that a life licence should be of two to five years duration at most. The features of their social worker's approach that ex-prisoners found most helpful were the interest they showed in their client, the fact that they were not pressurising and the fact that they were there when needed. Giving the impression that they did not care and having limited powers to positively influence offenders' material circumstances were the features of their social workers' approach that ex-prisoners found least helpful. Around two-thirds believed that their social worker had been helpful overall but just under a third felt that their involvement with social workers was too intrusive and time-consuming. Almost two-thirds of the sample felt they had gained nothing from the experience of throughcare. Just under half would have welcomed more proactive, practical support, particularly in relation to issues such as accommodation and employment.

Only seven offenders believed that offending might still be a problem which they wanted to address on release. Others felt that offending was an irrelevant issue frequently raised by the social worker, though nine ex-prisoners did not recall having discussed it at all. The majority of ex-prisoners (25) thought it unlikely that they would re-offend: only six believed that re-offending was likely. Twenty-five offenders believed that they were at less of risk of re-offending compared with when they were first released from custody. Throughcare was believed to have contributed significantly to the reduced risk of offending in four cases and to have contributed to some extent in nine others. Overall, then, throughcare was perceived to have had some impact on the likelihood of re-offending by 42 per cent (13 out of 31) of the sample. Other factors which had impacted positively upon the risk of recidivism included offenders' own motivation to avoid further offending and the significance of family and other personal relationships. More generally, ex-prisoners pointed to increased stability in their lives in areas such as employment or education, social contacts, increased maturity and control over former misuse of alcohol or drugs, issues which had similarly been stressed as significant by social workers.

CHAPTER SIX

THE EFFECTIVENESS OF COMMUNITY BASED THROUGHCARE IN SCOTLAND

INTRODUCTION

It has long been recognised that the throughcare of prisoners has been one of the areas of social work practice with offenders which has been least effectively developed both in Scotland and in England and Wales (McAllister et al, 1992). While some encouragement can be drawn from the present research it is clear that there is still, in some respects, some way to go. The present chapter considers some of the key findings of this study and discusses what appear to have been the main impediments to the development of a more effective community based throughcare service to discharged prisoners.

THE IMPACT OF NATIONAL STANDARDS ON COMMUNITY BASED THROUGHCARE

The National Standards provide a framework for the supervision of prisoners released under licence and for the provision of voluntary assistance to other prisoners in the 12 months following release. The National Standards recognise the importance of addressing ex-prisoners' practical, social and emotional problems as a prerequisite of effective throughcare practice. As Paragraph 92 of the throughcare standards (SWSG, 1991) indicates:

> Although many discharged prisoners may experience some emotional and social difficulties following release, practical problems concerning employment, accommodation and financial matters may be felt by many to constitute more pressing concerns. Unless these problems are addressed, the impact of supervision on the offender is likely to be minimal. The provision of advice, guidance and assistance (either directly or though the involvement of other specialists dealing with such issues) will be a key element in the social work task with many discharged prisoners.

In this respect, the guidance contained in the National Standards is consistent with the needs expressed by ex-prisoners themselves. The National Standards also attach importance to the role of community based throughcare as a means of addressing offending behaviour. Yet many ex-prisoners - especially those who had served lengthy sentences and who considered their offence to have been an isolated incident - did not believe further offending to be a relevant issue, to the point that they perceived their supervising social worker's emphasis upon it to be a distraction from other, more salient, concerns. Ex-prisoners emphasised, rather, the need for practical assistance to ease their transition back into society and re-integration into their local communities and believed that by focusing, often unnecessarily, upon their offending, social workers were less effective than they might otherwise have been.

Ex-prisoners' perceptions of the purpose of parole tended to accord with those of the Parole Board, which viewed practical assistance with resettlement in the community as the appropriate focus for parole supervision and which looked for evidence that the prisoner had, while in custody, addressed his or her offending behaviour as an indicator of suitability for parole (McAra, 1998). There would appear, on the face of it, to be a tension between the expectations of the Parole Board and ex-prisoners and the emphasis placed in the National Standards upon offending behaviour. The National Standards, however, unlike those which have been developed for probation supervision, stress the role of the social worker in managing offending behaviour as opposed to addressing offending behaviour. The former, which implies that the social work role should be to ensure that the ex-prisoner does not pose an unnecessary risk to the public, need not involve explicit discussion of offending behaviour unless it is necessary to minimise this risk. It is possible that in some instances social workers may have equated managing offending behaviour with addressing offending behaviour and by so doing have been diverted from the more appropriate task of providing practical and other support. Perhaps, therefore, greater attention needs to be given by supervising social workers to assessing the relative significance that needs to be attached to the ex-prisoner's offending as opposed to other problems to ensure that social work services can address the issue of public safety while meeting ex-prisoners' needs.

The fact that prison based social work is subject to a different funding mechanism from other social work services to the criminal justice system was said by social work managers to have had an adverse impact on the creation of an integrated throughcare service to prisoners, and disappointment was expressed that prison social work had only been included in local authority strategic plans in the most recent planning cycle. Furthermore, the introduction of agency status for the Scottish Prison Service had, it was argued, meant that energy that would otherwise have been devoted to service development in accordance with *Continuity Through Co-operation* (SPS/SWSG, 1989) was absorbed instead in securing a viable social work presence in prisons and providing a degree of continuity and security for prison based social work staff. The number and geographical spread of prisons was said to have prevented the development of the effective liaison and cooperation between local authorities which is recognised in *Continuity Through Co-operation* as essential to provide an appropriate continuity of service to prisoners and their families.

There appeared to be widespread lack of clarity among ex-prisoners as to the role of the prison based social worker both more generally and in relation to the resettlement process. Prison based social workers were regarded as less well placed than community based social workers to liaise effectively on behalf of the prisoner with outside agencies; in addition, their ability to provide a confidential service was viewed with a degree of scepticism by some prisoners. As such, prisoners tended to look to community based social workers to help them maintain or establish links with the communities to which they would return. Visits by community based social workers to serving prisoners were generally viewed in a positive light though the inaccessibility of many prisons was perceived as having prevented more regular contact during the sentence. The parole process, moreover, often resulted in prisoners being advised of their release date too soon prior to release for contact between the serving prisoner and the community based social worker to occur. As such, the notification of release dates often precluded, even in the case of those released on life licences, more careful planning and preparation for release.

The extent to which the National Standards for community based throughcare contribute to the effectiveness of services to released prisoners is difficult to assess since specific standards were not being met in a significant proportion of cases. The impact of local factors on the effectiveness of throughcare practice is considered in the following section.

THE IMPACT OF LOCAL FACTORS ON COMMUNITY BASED THROUGHCARE

Community based throughcare was acknowledged by social work managers in the participating authorities to be the area in which the least progress had been made in terms of policy implementation and the area in which the greatest difficulty had been encountered in meeting National Standards. A variety of explanations was offered for the relative lack of progress in this area of work. Throughcare had, it was suggested, historically been the "Cinderella" of social work with offenders. It was also an area of service delivery which was particularly resource intensive on account of the travel costs and staff time involved in visiting prisoners located in institutions across the country. The fact that throughcare was numerically less significant than other core areas of service provision, such as Social Enquiry Reports and probation, had also, it was suggested, contributed to its being afforded lower priority by social workers and managers. This also meant that there was a "gap in management expertise and staff expertise", particularly in rural areas where there was less opportunity to obtain experience of and develop skills in this area of work.

Probation services and academics in England and Wales have of late been engaged in debate over whether community based throughcare services can best be provided by dedicated teams, or whether it is possible for staff to gain expertise and experience in this area of work, and provide an effective service, if throughcare is competing on generic offender workers' caseloads with other service demands (Williams, 1995). Even in more densely populated areas, the costs of providing an effective throughcare service in line with National Standards was significantly increased if it required making contact with individual prisoners in institutions located at some considerable distance from their home area. The existence in Scott of a dedicated throughcare project, funded through the Urban Renewal Unit, was said by managers to have provided for a more efficient and more effective throughcare service to serving prisoners. Through being able to visit small groups of serving prisoners at one time the per capita costs of providing a more meaningful throughcare service were said to be significantly reduced.

The relatively small number of cases in each of the study areas prevent firm conclusions from being reached with respect to the effectiveness of throughcare practice across areas. It was apparent, however, that with respect to the timing of initial interviews and the frequency of contacts with ex-prisoners in the period following release, the National Standards were being met more consistently in Scott than in the other areas. Managers in Scott regularly sampled throughcare cases to monitor adherence to National Standards and to assess the quality of practice, feeding back the findings to social work staff. Whilst this mechanism appears to have encouraged practice which accords with National Standards (despite social workers in Scott occupying split posts and having additional responsibilities for other areas of work) its impact in terms of the effectiveness of throughcare practice is more difficult to discern. It may not be coincidental, however, that social workers in Scott more often focused upon the provision of various types of practical support to prisoners and this, as we have seen, was most highly valued by prisoners themselves.

In each of the participating authorities, throughcare was being accorded greater priority in more recent planning statements and strategic plans. Voluntary assistance was recognised as being the least well developed aspect of throughcare in Burns, but steps were being taken to rectify this situation through the identification by the court social worker of offenders sentenced to custody who would be eligible for voluntary aftercare. Particular efforts would be made to make contact with vulnerable or high risk groups of offenders (such as 16-17 year olds and sex offenders) with an offer of voluntary assistance approximately three months prior to release. In Bruce an attempt had been made to raise the profile of throughcare by including it in a formal review system and by according throughcare equal status to probation supervision in workload terms. It was, nevertheless, as a manager explained "still difficult getting over the perception of throughcare as less challenging for social workers and less relevant for clients".

THE SHORT TERM EFFECTIVENESS OF COMMUNITY BASED THROUGHCARE

Whilst the foregoing discussion may appear to suggest that community based throughcare was, in general, of limited effectiveness, there was clear evidence that the services provided to ex-prisoners had often made a positive contribution both to their re-integration into the community and to their risk of further offending behaviour. There was evidence of throughcare packages being tailored to the characteristics and needs of individual prisoners and the risk of further offending they were perceived to pose.

The ability of social workers to meet the immediate practical needs of ex-prisoners is, however, limited both by resources and by the social circumstances of prisoners on release, including limited opportunities for access to what Worrall (1995) has described as the "structural pre-conditions of social justice", including income, housing and employment. Each of the areas which participated in the present research had access to a range of other resources though the majority of work with ex-prisoners was undertaken by social workers themselves. The sense of frustration experienced by ex-prisoners when social workers are unable directly to influence their social circumstances in a positive direction might, however, be lessened if the latter convey clearly what they can realistically achieve and, more importantly, are seen as endeavouring, where possible, to provide the practical and emotional support necessary - including drawing, where relevant, upon other specialist agencies and services - to facilitate the ex-prisoner's re-integration into the community.

It appeared that in managing offending behaviour with ex-prisoners, social workers frequently found themselves in the position of maintaining an already low risk rather than reducing a potentially higher risk. Many ex-prisoners were considered not to present a risk of further offending when released from custody and community based throughcare could be judged a success if, at the very least, there was no evidence of increased risk to the public. This contrasts with probation supervision where the focus was clearly upon risk reduction and where the success of an order was perceived by supervising social workers in these terms (McIvor and Barry, 1998). This said, social workers believed that in some instances the ex-prisoner's risk of re-offending had further decreased since being released. This was most likely to have occurred when former prisoners had continued, while subject to community based throughcare, to gain further insights into their offending behaviour and had acquired skills which might equip them to deal more appropriately with situations which might previously have placed them at risk of offending behaviour.

Social work involvement following release was believed by social workers and prisoners alike to have had an impact on the risk of further offending in around two-fifths of cases, and there was some indication of an improvement in prisoners' social circumstances since being released from custody, though this could not always be attributed directly to the social work support and assistance they had received. There was, however, little evidence of re-offending during the period of community based throughcare and only two prisoners were recalled to prison as a consequence of having committed further offences. Both recalled prisoners had, however, been subject to parole licences with additional requirements attached suggesting that this category of ex-prisoner presents a greater risk to public safety than do those released under other statutory arrangements. This was reflected in the types of issues addressed with this group of prisoners and in social workers' views of the risk of re-offending presented by different categories of ex-prisoner following statutory supervision in the community.

It is likely that the level of recall will increase with the implementation of the new release arrangements for prisoners contained in the Prisoners and Criminal Procedures (Scotland) Act 1993. Prisoners released on licence will be subject to lengthier periods of parole supervision and many will be subject to supervision to which they have not been required to give their consent. The tension between managing the risk to the public and providing ex-prisoners with a range of practical support which eases their resettlement in the community is likely to be felt all the more acutely in respect of those prisoners who are subject to non-parole licence under the new arrangements and who are, arguably, among the most dangerous and least motivated individuals in the Scottish prison system.

CONCLUSIONS

The present study suggests that effective pockets of throughcare practice do exist. However, community based throughcare was viewed as less helpful than it might be by released prisoners. What appears to be required to improve the quality and effectiveness of community based throughcare is greater clarity regarding the objectives of throughcare practice, a level of resourcing which accurately reflects the requirements of an effective and comprehensive throughcare service, a clearer distinction between the role of prison based and community based social work staff in the period prior to release, improved communication and coordination between prison based and community based social workers, a longer time lapse between prisoners' notification of parole being granted and their release date, and a more consistent emphasis upon the practical needs of prisoners on release. Dedicated throughcare teams might be a solution but they are unlikely to be viable other than in areas of relatively high population density. Another possibility, which received some support from ex-prisoners themselves, was the use of throughcare volunteers, not as a means of downgrading the throughcare process, but as a means of linking ex-prisoners to individuals in the community who had both the time and the local knowledge to provide assistance and support of a more proactive kind.

ANNEX I

INFORMATION FROM CASE FILES

The following information was gathered from the social work case files of individual ex-prisoners in the sample:

- the characteristics of the offender (including age, gender, previous criminal history[18])

- details of the sentence imposed (including the number of offences, the nature and gravity rating[19] of the main offence and the length of custodial sentence)

- the ex-prisoner's circumstances on release (including accommodation, employment, marital status and family commitments)

- the nature of throughcare arrangements (type of throughcare, nature of any additional requirements and duration of supervision)

- the dates of pre-release meetings with the prisoner and contact with the prisoner's family

- issues addressed by community based and prison based social workers prior to release

- areas of work identified for post-release services both prior to and following release

- services provided during community based throughcare contact, including the method of intervention (individual or group) and the nature of service providers

- the frequency, nature and location of contacts with the ex-prisoner

- the numbers of reviews, their outcomes and participants

- the number of supervising social workers and reasons for a change of social worker

- the number of formal warnings issued and details of any notifications (and their outcomes) to the Scottish Office Home and Health Department (now The Scottish Office Home Department)

- the reason for termination of contact with the ex-prisoner

- the number, nature and outcomes of further offences during the throughcare period

- the social circumstances of ex-prisoners at the end of throughcare contact (including accommodation and employment).

---

[18] The Scottish Criminal Record Office provided details of previous convictions to ensure that this information was both comprehensive and consistent across study areas.

[19] The gravity rating employed by Creamer et al (1993) in the calculation of a risk of custody score was employed. This assigns offences a gravity rating of one to 5, with the least serious offences being assigned a gravity rating of one and the most serious a gravity rating of 5.

ANNEX II

SOCIAL WORKERS' QUESTIONNAIRES

The social workers' questionnaires invited them to give their views on the following issues in individual cases:

- the main areas of work in the case as defined by the social worker and by the ex-prisoner
- the objectives of community based throughcare and the extent to which they had been achieved
- the ex-prisoner's motivation to address his/her offending and other problems
- the ex-prisoner's response to throughcare and factors which had influenced that response
- the features of throughcare which ex-prisoners had found most and least helpful
- the risk of continued offending and any change in risk since release from custody
- where relevant, the contribution that throughcare supervision or support, as opposed to other factors, had made to achieving a reduction in risk
- any other comments about the effectiveness of throughcare supervision in that particular case

ANNEX III

INTERVIEWS WITH EX-PRISONERS

Interviews with ex-prisoners who had been in receipt of community based throughcare focused upon the following areas:

- contact with the community based social worker prior to release (including the frequency and timing of visits, issues discussed, help provided and views about the usefulness of such contact). In the case of those who had not received a visit from their social worker while in custody, questions sought to establish whether such contact would have been helpful and what form it might most usefully have taken

- in the case of statutory supervision, the timing of initial contact with the social worker on release and the clarity with which the expectations of the licence were explained

- in the case of voluntary assistance, how and why ex-prisoners contacted the social work department and the types of help they expected to receive

- in all cases the types of problems respondents experienced on release from prison, their motivation to address them and the help they received

- motivation to address offending, whether and how it was discussed by the social worker and the impact of such discussion on ex-prisoners' understanding of their offending and their motivation not to re-offend

- the nature of any additional requirements, what they were supposed to achieve and how helpful they were

- the frequency and length of contact with the social worker, the relationship established with the social worker and the social worker's approach

- reasons for any non-compliance or recall and response to having been recalled

- general views about the experience of throughcare and its effectiveness, including what respondents had hoped to achieve while in receipt of throughcare and the extent to which these expectations were fulfilled

- views about further offending including the risk of further offending, whether that risk had changed since being released from custody and, if it had, the contribution that throughcare, as opposed to other factors, had made to achieving a reduction in risk. Where relevant, respondents were also asked to indicate what other factors had made it less likely that they would re-offend.

REFERENCES

Brown, L., Levy, L. and McIvor, G. (1998) *Social Work and Criminal Justice: The National and Local Context.* Edinburgh: The Stationery Office.

Brown, L. and Levy, L. (1998) *Social Work and Criminal Justice: Sentencer Decision Making.* Edinburgh: The Stationery Office.

Creamer, A., Ennis, E. and Williams, B. (1993) *The Dunscore: A method for predicting risk of custody within the Scottish context and its use in social enquiry practice,* Dundee: Department of Social Work, University of Dundee.

Duffee, D. E. and Clark, D. (1985) The frequency and classification of the needs of offenders in community settings, *Journal of Criminal Justice,* 13, 243-68.

McAllister, D., Bottomely, K. and Leibling, A. (1992) *From Custody to Community: Throughcare for Young Offenders,* Aldershot: Avebury.

McAra, L (1998) *Social Work and Criminal Justice: Early Arrangements.* Edinburgh: The Stationery Office.

McAra, L. (1998a) *Social Work and Criminal Justice: Parole Board Decision Making.* Edinburgh: The Stationery Office.

McIvor, G. and Barry, M. (1998) *Social Work and Criminal Justice: Probation.* Edinburgh: The Stationery Office.

Paterson, F and Tombs, J. (1998) *Social Work and Criminal Justice: The Impact of Policy.* Edinburgh: The Stationery Office.

Rifkind, M. (1989) Penal policy: the way ahead, *The Howard Journal of Criminal Justice,* 28, 81-90.

Social Work Services Group (1991) *National Objectives and Standards for Social Work Services in the Criminal Justice System,* Edinburgh: The Scottish Office.

Social Work Services Group (1993) *Social Work Services in the Criminal Justice System: Summary of National Objectives and Standards,* Edinburgh: The Scottish Office.

SPS/SWSG (1989) *Continuity Through Co-operation: A National Framework of Policy and Practice Guidance for Social Work in Scottish Penal Establishments,* Edinburgh: Scottish Prison Service/Social Work Services Group.

Williams, B. (1995) Social work with prisoners, in G. McIvor (Ed.) *Research Highlights in Social Work No. 26: Working with Offenders,* London: Jessica Kingsley.

Worrall, A. (1995) Gender, criminal justice and probation, in G. McIvor (Ed.) *Research Highlights in Social Work No. 26: Working with Offenders,* London: Jessica Kingsley.

Printed in Scotland for The Stationery Office Limited
J37711, C7, 2/98, CCN 003808